The spiritual dimension is prob~~_~~ ~~_~~ sion of life that one faces as death nears, and yet few resources exist to provide key insights into this process, until now. This text offers profound and practical insights to caregivers, family members, and pastoral-care workers in how to assist the terminally ill with the inevitable questions, concerns, and unique situations that arise during the dying process. Drawing upon dramatic real-life encounters with the dying, William Griffith leaves no subject adrift as he tackles such topics as how to seek forgiveness, how to give permission to someone to die, and how to allow the inner beauty of an individual to shine forth. If you have ever visited a terminally ill person and felt an awkward silence, this text provides the remedy. I strongly recommend this text to anyone seeking more insight into this topic that will eventually face us all.

—Dr. Jeff Woods
Associate General Secretary, American Baptist Churches USA

William Griffith's work as an after-hours chaplain for hospice has given him access to the very personal and unique stories of patients and their loved ones. His interpretation of these experiences is sensitive, insightful, and inspiring…a wonderful contribution to our understanding of the role of faith in these profound moments.

—Kathy Melamed, CISW
Director, Counseling and Support Services,
Hospice of the Valley, Phoenix, AZ

Life isn't measured by the breaths you take but by the moments that take your breath away. William Griffith shares breath-taking stories that *teach* your head, *touch* your heart, and *train* your people. School your skills by breathing in these sacred stories!

—Dr. Dick Hamlin
Lutheran Clergyman, Spiritual Director,
and Mentor with The Hudson Institute

More than a Parting Prayer is an insightful, refreshing look at life and death. William Griffith helps pastors to be better care providers to families who are dealing with the reality of death and grief in their lives. This book is rooted in the understanding that there is a deeply spiritual dimension to all of us. What a great privilege: to be able to help people finish living so that they can die peacefully.

—*The Rev. Dr. Rollin Strode*
Lead Pastor, First Baptist Church of Greenacres, Bakersfield, CA

As someone who grew up in a religious environment that emphasized being a faithful "witness," it is refreshing to read intimate stories from someone who has so obviously practiced the art of "with-ness." For everyone who dares to fall into step with those who journey into the "Valley of the Shadow"— even seasoned caregivers—this book will be a helpful companion, providing rich insight and leaving its own indelible footprints.

—*The Rev. Jim Guyer*
Parish Associate for Congregational Care, Cedar Heights Community Presbyterian Church, Cedar Falls, Iowa

More than a Parting Prayer is not just another "how-to" book on coping with death. William Griffith expertly weaves the spiritual experiences of those he has served together with profound truths we can all apply to our own journey of life and death. He has created a tapestry of inspiration and life's lessons for us all to learn and apply to our lives.

—*Lee E. Arp, Faith Community Outreach Coordinator/*
Pastoral Counselor, Hospice of the Valley, Phoenix, AZ

As a supervisor of a group of hospice pastoral counselors, I have often wished someone were writing an account of the uniquely sensitive and meaningful encounters shared in our discussions. William Griffith has done just that regarding his pastoral encounters. In a style that touches us at a spiritual level, he wonderfully relates numerous and diverse moments of pastoral care with dying persons and their families. He avoids religious dogmatism and, true to his purpose, leaves footprints of persons who connected and found new definitions of hope as they walked briefly together.

—*Gary Kriege, M.A., Diplomate in the American Association of Pastoral Counselors and Executive Director of Arizona Interfaith Counseling*

In his new book, *More than a Parting Prayer,* the Rev. Dr. William Griffith offers chaplains and, indeed all who serve persons facing death, a rich and valuable resource. He writes as a Christian minister with a doctor of ministry degree, as a hospice pastoral counselor who has served over 1,400 dying patients and their families, and as one who has experienced the pain of loss of loved ones of his own. Out of his training, faith, sensitivity—and, I suspect, the inspiration and support of the Holy Spirit—he has written an insightful book that will assist others, whether believers or nonbelievers, professionals or volunteers, as well as family members, accompany and serve those who are in their spiritual journey of dying. I highly recommend it to them.

—*Msgr. Edward J. Ryle*
Retired Director, Arizona Catholic Conference, Phoenix, AZ

more than a parting prayer
lessons in care-giving for the dying

WILLIAM H. GRIFFITH

JUDSON PRESS
PUBLISHERS SINCE 1824

Valley Forge, Pennsylvania

more than a parting prayer
lessons in care-giving for the dying

Judson Press has made every effort to trace the ownership of all quotes. In the event of a question arising from the use of a quote, we regret any error made and will be pleased to make the necessary correction in future printings and editions of this book.

Unless otherwise indicated, Bible quotations in this volume are from the New Revised Standard Version of the Bible, copyright © 1989 by the Division of Christian Education of the National Council of Churches of Christ in the United States of America. Used by permission. All rights reserved. Other quotes are from the *New International Version*, copyright © 1973, 1978, 1984. Used by permission of Zondervan Bible Publishers (NIV).

Library of Congress Cataloging-in-Publication Data

Griffith, William H.
  More than a parting prayer : lessons in care-giving for the dying / William H. Griffith.— 1st ed.
    p. cm.
  ISBN 0-8170-1480-2 (alk. paper)
  1. Church work with the terminally ill. 2. Death—Religious aspects—Christianity. 3. Terminal care—Religious aspects—Christianity. I. Title.
  BV4460.6.G75 2005
  259'.4175—dc22

                                                                        2004024628

Printed in the U.S.A.

10 09 08 07 06 05 04

10 9 8 7 6 5 4 3 2 1

*To the memory of the spiritual journeys
of three members of my family:*

*My mother, Norma B. Griffith,
March 11, 1914–April 26, 2003*

*My sister-in-law, Clarice L. Dietrich,
February 3, 1937–November 2, 2002*

*My sister-in-law, Sarah A. Dietrich,
October 9, 1954–October 5, 2003*

Contents

Preface

SHARED PERSONAL STORIES provide honest insights into the feelings and emotions of those who tell them. When those stories are told by a dying person, we discover lessons that cannot be taught by anyone else. I have been privileged, as an on-call chaplain with Hospice of the Valley in Phoenix, Arizona, to sit by the beds of dying patients and their families, listen to them share their hopes as well as their sorrows, and learn from them. Now I want to share what I have learned with both professionals and laypersons who want to know more about caring for those who are dying.

If there's one main lesson I have learned from these experiences, it is that no one has all the answers, but that's okay. What the dying want more than answers is another person's presence. They want to know that someone cares and to experience that caring in a way that meets their particular needs.

Any person who wants to journey as a caregiver with a dying patient will know uncertainty as he or she enters into a relationship with the patient. Some of the words that define that relationship are *honesty, vulnerability,* and *risk-taking.* Add to these the emotions of sorrow, joy, sadness, fear, hope, and grief and it is easy to understand why people often feel inadequate to begin such a relationship. It is my hope that the lessons learned from these stories will provide enough encouragement for some to be convinced that it's worth a try.

Reflection questions for personal or group use are included in the appendix.

William H. Griffith

Acknowledgments

I AM INDEBTED to all of those families who have welcomed me into their lives and have become my teachers. The names of the people in the stories in this book, in most cases, except for those in chapter 23, have been changed out of respect for their privacy. The family named in chapter 23 gave me permission to use their names.

Thanks also to my daughter, Karen G. Kreider, who did a fine job of improving her dad's manuscript. She was more than willing to put to good use her college degree in writing. I did make or approve changes after her editing, however, so if there are errors, I take full responsibility.

I would never have begun this effort without special encouragement from my friend Bob Rhude, who in listening to my stories insisted that I write them down, and also Melanie Rigney, who, after reading my earliest stories, provided the needed encouragement for me to prepare the manuscript.

My wife, Lois, was always the first person to hear these stories told, and her affirming response helped convince me that they were worth sharing.

I am especially grateful to those who read the manuscript and agreed to write an endorsement. No one read the manuscript more often or more thoroughly than my agent, Barbara Neighbors Deal. I appreciate her fine work. I also appreciate Randy Frame and the staff at Judson Press for their attention to detail.

There are many others who provided me with encouragement and helped me make the contacts to find the right people to help me turn a dream into a book. Thanks to all of you.

Introduction

I HAVE A FRIEND who years ago gave up teaching high school history and made a career change. He interviewed with a national company for the position of director of sales, head of the department that trained all of the company's national sales force. During the interview, the person from the human resources department looked over the biographical information sheet and asked my friend, "Have you ever been a salesman?"

My friend responded, "No, sir, I have not."

The interviewer then asked, "What gives you the confidence to apply for this position to teach others how to sell if you have never been in sales?"

My friend calmly replied, "Sir, I taught the Civil War for fifteen years, but I never fought in it."

My friend got the job, and it was because of his honesty.

When it comes to helping those who are dying, I believe that what my friend said during that interview is also true for caregivers. None of us has died, so we can't know how it feels. But all of us are interested in learning how to provide better care for those who are dying.

Death isn't usually a subject that people feel comfortable discussing. Being informed that someone you know and love has less than six months to live is disturbing news. Processing that information includes redefining your relationship with the one who is dying and the members of his or her family. *What will I say when I see her? Should I call? Should I visit? What will we talk about?* These are only some of the questions that race through our minds. We experience a mixture of sadness and sorrow as we begin to wrestle with the meaning of losing someone we value. We have begun to grieve the person's loss even before he or she dies, and we are uncertain how we ought to respond.

This journey into the valley of the shadow also creates anxiety for both laypersons and clergy who choose to be caregivers. Each must begin to sort out how he or she will relate to the dying and to their family members. Each person needs to be in touch with his or her own human condition, fears, and faith values. Yet this is one of those life experiences for which few have had academic training, and therefore few feel they know what to expect or do. The absence of such training, however, does not remove the need to respond. Because of our relationship with the person who is dying, we know that we will have to make decisions that reflect our desire to care for him or her.

For clergy who provide pastoral care for a congregation, care-giving will mean more than a bedside chat and a parting prayer. The most effective pastoral care demands an awareness and a sensitivity to how the shattering news has altered every relationship in the dying person's life, including his or her relationship with the pastor. A layperson who is serving as a member of a church caregiving ministry needs the same awareness and sensitivity and must consciously shape his or her relationship with the dying person in light of this.

Lesson #1: Being Is Doing

Both clergy and laypersons will experience frustration over their inability to change the circumstances of the dying person's situation. The desire to want to "do something" will be strong, and the realization that there is little to do may cause the caregiver to want to distance him- or herself from the person who is dying. It is at this point that the caregiver must learn the first lesson in providing care for the dying, and it is this: Being is doing.

Simply being with the person who is dying may cause the caregiver internal turmoil, because it may feel like nothing is being done to change the situation. It is important for the caregiver to realize that doing is not what the dying patient expects. The person who is dying has already been confronted with the medical diagnosis and is not looking to any caregiver to change that. What he needs is someone to be with him. He doesn't need a person with answers; he simply needs a person.

Lesson #2: Be Honest

Once we are willing to simply be with the person who is dying, we must then struggle with "What should I say?" It's one thing to agree to be with the dying person but another to worry about saying the wrong thing. The best way to proceed is found in a second important lesson: Be honest with your feelings of inadequacy. Conveying this feeling to the dying person is not a sign of weakness on your part, but one of vulnerability. You are not alone: The dying person doesn't know what to say either.

Feelings of inadequacy can be conveyed through the sharing of an embrace and tears, or they can be verbalized. When such sharing takes place, both caregiver and patient have reached a common ground of honesty and vulnerability, and the dying person will know that the caregiver does indeed care. Once this level of honesty has been reached, the journey together has begun.

Lesson #3: Redefine Hope

Because a terminal diagnosis carries with it a sense of hopelessness, it is important that those who relate to and care for the dying also know a third important lesson: Listen for ways to redefine hope. The person who is processing a terminal diagnosis must not be robbed of hope. Once she has been convinced that there is no cure for her illness and she no longer hopes for one, she needs to be able to hope for what is measurable and achievable. This kind of hope, which draws her into a future that has been redefined, gives her reason to look ahead.

Providing hope must not be overlooked simply because of the patient's physical decline and loss of independence. It is believed that hearing takes no energy and that a dying person may hear even when she cannot lift her eyelids. In light of this, the caregiver would do well to provide the patient with any information that relates to what she has been hoping for, even when she seems to be beyond actual communication. She will be more ready to welcome death when she knows that her hopes have been fulfilled.

One Christmas week, an elderly woman in one of our palliative care units (a hospice facility for dying patients) shared her hope with her daughter that she wanted to live until Christmas. Since Christmas was only four days away, the staff agreed that this was realistic. But the woman died two days before Christmas, and her daughter was distraught because she believed her mother's hope had not been fulfilled. However, when I counseled with her, she recounted how happy her mother had been the night of the staff Christmas party, when the church carolers came by to sing for her and Santa gave her a kiss. I realized that the daughter had left that evening unaware that, for her mother, Christmas had actually arrived during that party. It was not a date on the calendar that defined her hope; it was the familiar rituals of the season. She had experienced them and was then content to let go. When I helped the daughter to understand this, she experienced a sense of relief and comfort. Her hope, too, had been redefined.

I invite everyone, layperson or clergy, to sit with me by the bedside, to listen to the stories that follow, and to learn about what is important to the dying. Many of these stories will more than once reflect the principles outlined above. My intention is not to be repetitive, but to reinforce these important principles so they take root. Not all of these stories end with easy answers or conclusions, but such is the nature of this kind of care-giving ministry.

My hope is that by encountering these stories, not only will you gain insight into how to care for the dying, but you will also get more in touch with your own feelings and comfort (or discomfort) zones. For in so doing, we are in a better position to learn and grow and become more effective as caregivers.

chapter 1

From Restlessness to Peace

Death brings you a choice.
It can lead you
to the edge of the abyss.
Or you can build a bridge
that will span the chasm.
　　　　　　　　—Earl A. Grollman

JOHN WAS SIXTY-FOUR YEARS OLD and dying, and he was anxious. He asked to talk with a pastoral counselor on a Saturday evening, so I was called. I arrived at 8:30 p.m. and was greeted by his wife and introduced to his daughter, son, and sister-in-law. The living room had become a storage space for the bedroom furniture that had been moved so that a hospital bed could be set up for John in the more comfortable and familiar surroundings of his home.

I was immediately escorted into John's room. He was awake and made eye contact with me as I walked toward his bed. He slowly lifted his thin arm and extended his hand to shake mine. I introduced myself, and he thanked me for coming. I asked him what it was that he was concerned about. His wife started to leave the room so that we could talk, but, looking at her, John said, "You can stay." She sat on the other side of the hospital bed and held his hand.

We again made eye contact, and John said to me, "I don't know what to do."

I didn't want to assume that I knew what he was referring to, nor did I want to guess, so I responded by asking, "What to do about what, John?"

He closed his eyes and in a soft, weak voice said, "Is there something I need to do to die?"

I said, "John, I'll bet you have been the kind of guy who always wanted to get the job done the right way." His wife smiled, and John nodded in agreement. "We've been raised to be doers, haven't we John?" He nodded again. He had his eyes closed, and after some moments of silence he opened them and looked at me. I asked, "Before you die, John, is there anything at all that you feel you'd like to do or anyone you'd like to see?"

Softly he replied, "No."

Again there was silence among the three of us until I said, "Well, then the hardest thing you have to do is wait, and it's my guess that since you're a doer, waiting isn't something you enjoy. We doers want to get on with what must be done. Your wife and family share this frustration with you. Although they do things for you by providing you with food and drink, what they might not know is that what you really appreciate is what your wife is doing right now—sitting by your bed and holding your hand and being with you." He nodded slightly, and a tear formed at the corner of his eye. His wife handed him a tissue, and he touched it to the tear.

"This isn't a time to do, John; it's a time to be," I said. "Being is everything. Right now being with you is all your family can do for you. Being with you is what God promises also. Are you aware that God loves you and is with you?"

"Yes," he said.

Then I offered, "John, that's what the wonderful promise is in the twenty-third Psalm, where we read, 'Even though I walk through the valley of the shadow of death, I will fear no evil, for you are with me' (23:4). It doesn't say that at such a time the shepherd—God—will do anything for us; it simply says that he will be with us. At the time of our lives when we can't do for ourselves and we face this mystery we call death, we can claim the promise of our God being with us. All I can do for you is be with you and remind you of that promise. All you can do is claim that promise as being true for you. Do you claim that promise?"

John's eyes opened, and he said, "Yes, I do." His wife now had tears in her eyes.

I asked John if he would like me to pray with him. He quickly agreed. I offered a prayer, then spoke some parting words of blessing and hope and left the bedroom.

As I stood in the living room by the front door, John's wife apologized for the mess of furniture that was stacked in the room. I reassured her that it was a wonderful symbol of her love and devotion to her husband. The cluttered room spoke loudly that she would do anything she could to make John's last days as comfortable as possible. I affirmed the love and support the family was providing for John, and I reminded them that their being with him was everything they could do.

As I turned to leave, John's wife put her hand on my shoulder and said, "Thank you. He seems so much more at peace now."

As I left the house and reached for the keys to my truck, I kept hearing those words in my head, and I marveled at what had happened during my brief, thirty-minute visit with John: A dying man's restlessness had been transformed into a new understanding and sense of contentment.

Lessons for Caregivers

When the dying person has had all of her wishes, desires, or hopes fulfilled, she can then become frustrated with waiting for the end to come. That waiting is in itself an experience for which we are so little prepared. It isn't that life has no experiences of waiting that teach us the fundamentals. We've all waited in the long checkout line in the grocery store or taken a number at the license bureau, but that waiting is simply a delay that keeps us from something else that is more exciting. Waiting to die is the ultimate "check-out" line, and we've never done that before.

What we do once we have entered that "check-out" line will depend, to a great degree, on how we have lived and what we have valued. John valued his family, and they were present to share the waiting with him. His religious beliefs provided him with sufficient assurance and faith that there was something more beyond the ultimate "check-out" line. He was able to verbalize this belief, and when a dying person gives verbal expression to his faith, he is not only validating the value of the faith by which he lived but also communicating to loved ones a state of readiness to die. Is it any wonder that John was "so much more at peace" after verbalizing his readiness?

Dying people have feelings just like everyone else, and they also have a need to share those feelings. Often their restlessness during their final days is in some way an attempt to communicate an unfulfilled need at a time when their every need must be met by someone else. They must be fed, bathed, medicated, and even turned over in bed, and their physical inactivity may so define their limitations for us, their caregivers, that we might fail to see or sense their struggle and their need for help at the emotional level. A dying person's journey will not seem as lonely if he has someone with whom he can talk and who sees to his emotional needs.

Remember that caring for the spouse and other family members of the dying is also important. Sometimes that may be as simple as pointing to the inconvenience of a cluttered room as an affirming symbol of the extent of the family's love for the dying. Family members need to be encouraged, and their caring needs to be affirmed.

chapter 2

The Mysterious Power of Hope

▨▨▨

Mystery is not an argument for the existence of God; mystery is an experience of the existence of God. Very much like suffering and joy, mystery can often be that place in which we come to know better who God is, and who we are.

—*Peter J. Gomes*

TOM WAS A NEW PATIENT at our hospice, and I stopped by his room to tell him about our pastoral counseling services. After introducing myself and meeting one of Tom's sons and his wife, I turned to Tom and asked, "How are you doing?"

He peered through eyes that were deeply set in the sockets of his cheekbones and said, "That's a stupid question. I wouldn't be here if I were doing OK, now would I?" The twinkle in his eye told me that Tom had a very dry sense of humor.

I replied, "We both know how you're doing and why you're here, but I want to know how you are doing today, under these circumstances."

Tom thought for a moment, then replied with slow, hesitant speech, "Bill, have you ever been here when someone has died?"

I nodded and said, "Yes, I have."

"How did they do it?" Tom asked.

I realized that this was a serious question, so I said, "Tell me just what it is you want to know."

He said, "I just want to know what I can do to die."

"Well, Tom," I began, "I'm not sure I can give you a formula that works every time. From my experience, there seems to be one controlling force that a dying person has, and it is that part of us that relates to our will. It is a fact that when a person wills or wishes to live for a certain event, say a birthday or an anniversary, he often does so, and then he dies soon after." This being the year 2000, I told Tom that it had been documented that more people than usual died just after the start of the new year and that it was thought that they wanted to live to enter the new millennium. "Let me ask you this," I continued. "Are there any reasons for you to want to live beyond today?"

Tom responded quickly and without much hesitation, but still with his slowness of speech, "Yes, there is. I have a daughter coming from Utah today and a son flying in from Maine on Sunday. I want to see them. I haven't seen them in a long time."

"That sounds to me like a pretty strong reason," I said. "When you get to see them, will that mean that your house is in order and there are no more loose ends to tie up?"

"Exactly. They're going to be here over the Memorial Day weekend and then for a few extra days. I'm anxious to see them."

"It sounds like it's pretty important business to take care of. What you are doing is hoping for something to happen. Even in your dying condition, you are able to hope. It is that hope that I was speaking about when I said a person can wish for something to happen before he or she dies. Your hope isn't measured in years or even weeks but in a few days. That is a powerful force that can enable a person to hold on until he's reached that certain goal. I will hope with you."

Tom smiled and said, "Thank you." I looked at his son and daughter-in-law and asked if they would like to share a prayer together with us. They agreed, and we held hands while I asked God to grant to Tom the desire of his heart to see all of his children over the weekend.

The following day was Sunday, and I was back in Tom's hospital unit. I stopped in to see him, and he introduced me to his daughter, who had arrived from Utah. He said that his son would arrive that evening. He seemed very satisfied.

Later, as I sat at the nursing desk filling out my reports, a nurse who had noticed me visiting with Tom said, "Guess what Tom told me this morning during his bath?"

"What did he tell you?" I asked.

"He said that his children were all going to be here with him over Memorial Day and through Wednesday, and that he was going to die on Thursday."

I smiled and shared with the nurse the conversation I'd had with Tom the day before. We both knew that there was no guarantee Tom's prediction would come true, but we were both hopeful that he would get his wish.

In the end, Tom didn't die immediately after his hope to see his children was fulfilled. He lived for six more days before finally passing into eternity. But when he died he knew that he was ready.

Lessons for Caregivers

Tom's question sounded very much like the one John asked me in the last chapter. Caregivers may find that dying patients often ask similar questions, but it is important not to assume that the questions always mean the same thing. When I pursued Tom's question I discovered that, unlike John, Tom still had some reasons to live before he was ready to die. By helping a dying person to focus on some specific reason that he or she would like to live, we provide a measurable time span for that hope. It is a fact that many deaths have occurred after the patients have celebrated some special event. Hope, in some mysterious way, energizes the will and gives the person a sense of control over the timing of his or her death.

Just what the dying patient hopes for is very personal. Tom's hope—to see someone who was very special to him—is a hope that is commonly expressed by the dying. In Tom's case the hope was to see his son and daughter who lived at a distance and who had specific plans to visit him at a specific time. Because their plans were made, Tom could think in terms of the number of days until they arrived and could anticipate his hope being fulfilled in the time they would share together.

The mysterious process of closure that Tom experienced reminds us of how important it is to not rob the dying patient of hope but rather help to redefine it. When the dying express any wish or desire, they are giving us helpful information as to what or whom they value, as well as the time frame of living in which they expect to find meaning. It is the anticipated marker on the calendar (anniversary, birthday, holiday, or visit) that they define as important, that may trigger the will and give them some sense of control. Such control is very important to people who are totally dependent on others for everything. Listening for what is wished or hoped for helps the caregiver know how best to support and care for that person.

chapter 3

Confession Cleans the Slate

Death makes the question of God an empirically testable question. Death makes the abstract God-question concrete. Instead of "Is there a God?" the question becomes "Will I see God?" It is a dramatic thought, the thought of meeting God at death. Death gives life to the God-question.

—*Peter J. Kreeft*

KELLY WAS A DIVORCED, forty-two-year-old mother of two who was dying of breast cancer that had spread to her brain. I met her one morning after a nurse suggested to me that she might appreciate a visit. I entered the hospital room and introduced myself. Kelly took a long look at me and then said, "Sit on the bed; I don't bite!"

I sat down and began, as I did with most patients, to ask about the journey of Kelly's illness. Her story was filled with statements of hopelessness, abandonment, and despair as she told me of how she had failed as a mother to show her children the way to live to please God. She told me how her ex-husband's mother had been very good about taking the girls to church and that they were turning out good "in spite of me," as she put it.

I asked Kelly what her spiritual journey was like, and she cracked a sarcastic grin and said, "It ain't been much of a journey." She told me that she had gone through classes at church to become a member, but it was just something she did. "It obviously didn't make much of a difference, did it?" she asked.

We sat in silence, looking at each other. In those moments, I sensed that Kelly was desperately reaching out, hoping to hear a word that could remove all the "junk" that had found its way into her life to that point. She shrugged her shoulders and shook her head. Then, as tears began forming in her eyes, she said, "I'm a hopeless mess."

I responded, "Kelly, although that's the way you feel at this moment, I assure you that God loves you. As long as you have breath, you have the chance to make things right with God."

Again, she shook her head from side to side, saying, "It's hard for me to believe that, as much as I have messed up my life and the lives of others, God could have enough time to make it right."

I reached out to take her hand and said, "Kelly, I'm here to tell you that it really doesn't take God a lot of time to make it right. It just takes your wanting God to do that."

She responded, "You make it sound easy."

"That's because it is, Kelly. Anything is easy when someone else does it all, and that's what God has done. There really isn't anything you can do except confess all of this unworthiness you've been telling me about and ask God to wipe the slate clean."

As the tears continued to well up in her eyes, she said, "I want to do that."

She reached out her other hand to me, and I held both of them as we sat together on her bed. She bowed her head and closed her eyes and began praying her own prayer of confession. She unloaded all of those years of sinful baggage she had been carrying around. She let God know how awful she had treated him and how abandoned she felt. She pleaded for forgiveness and then said, "Amen."

I followed with a prayer of assurance, thanking God for being faithful to his promises to forgive us and to welcome us home again. When I finished, we lifted our heads, and I saw the face of one whose burdens had been lifted. Kelly's eyes were sparkling. She had experienced the joy of divine forgiveness. She squeezed my hands, then put her arms around my neck and whispered,

"Thank you. I've needed to do that for a long time."

We talked for another twenty minutes, and I reminded Kelly of God's wonderful grace and of the gift of time he had given her so that she could come to this experience.

The next weekend Kelly began to fail physically, but her transformed spirit was obvious to all who visited at her bedside. She affirmed to me her continued joy about being forgiven and about her chance to make things right with her family.

The next weekend she was not alert, but family members were at her bedside, and I spoke with them about the experience I had shared with Kelly. They said that she had told them about it, and they were all glad. It gave them all the sense of closure they needed. They and others who visited Kelly in her last few weeks witnessed a weakening body, but one that housed a transformed soul.

Lessons for Caregivers

"Death-bed conversions" are often spoken of in ways that imply judgment on the dying person for waiting so long to be reconciled with God. Most people (such as Kelly) who have experienced such a conversion would agree that the experience of transforming joy is a bittersweet thing. Kelly was the first to regret that she had not met God sooner, but she was also grateful that God was gracious in giving her the time she needed to experience forgiveness.

There's no way to document the movement of the Spirit in another person's life, but in Kelly's situation there were family members who had been praying for her before I ever spoke with her. The caregiver's opportunity to share hope with a dying patient will often be part of a larger picture that includes others who have been praying or otherwise caring for the patient.

There are spiritual journeys that are full of sadness and despair, failure and regret, hopelessness and guilt. The unresolved baggage of a lifetime is a burden that is carried into the final miles of the journey. The dying may have memories that haunt them. Their pasts are filled with lost opportunities, and the weight of guilt convinces them that they do not deserve another chance. There may be no medicine for them except the love of a caregiver. Amidst all this, caregivers have the opportunity to share the good news that there is still hope.

Knowing that her days were few, Kelly redeemed them by being reconciled with her children and family. Conversations of love and words of forgiveness provided meaningful memories that the family will always treasure. Caregivers with good news to share can make a difference.

chapter 4

Learning to See the Heart

Death and grief are terrorizing experiences. We are bankrupt emotionally. We stand at a ground zero that makes us question if we will ever be able to rebuild our lives. When Jesus offered thanks at the tomb of Lazarus, the results were miraculous in raising Lazarus, and when we offer thanks at such a moment something miraculous also happens. No, our loved one does not rise from the grave, but in some miraculous way WE do.
—William H. Griffith

I CONDUCTED MY FIRST funeral/memorial service as a hospice pastoral counselor on a Sunday afternoon. I was substituting for one of the weekday counselors who was not available. The only information given to me, besides the telephone number of the widow, was that the deceased was a fifty-eight-year-old Harley Davidson biker and that the memorial service was to be conducted in the man's home.

I telephoned the widow of the deceased and introduced myself, and we agreed on 2:00 p.m. on Sunday as the time for the service. I asked her if she had anything she wanted me to be sure to include in the service, but she simply told me that I was to do whatever I needed to do. The man's daughter would write something for me to read, if that was OK.

On the day of the service, I arrived in the South Phoenix neighborhood, located the correct street, and began looking for the address I had written down. The neighborhood's property values had long since expired. Chain-link fences enclosed many of the front yards, and the match-box-size houses had carports that were filled more with broken furniture than with cars. Trucks and cars were parked where grass once grew. In front of the house with the number that matched the one on my yellow notepad, a car without wheels sat hoisted up on four concrete blocks.

I parked my white '87 Volkswagen camper/van, retrieved my Bible and notes from my attaché case, got out, locked the doors, and crossed the street to the house. The gate of the four-foot-high chain-link fence was unlocked, so I was able to enter. Two black Harley motorcycles rested on their kickstands nearby. Two aluminum lawn chairs, with broken green and yellow seats, leaned against the house.

I stepped up onto the concrete slab at the front of the house and knocked on the aluminum screen door that was missing the upper portion of the screen. The door opened, and I was greeted by a woman I assumed to be the widow. This tall, slender woman with hair dyed coal black and ruby-red lips invited me in as I handed her my hospice card and introduced myself.

Every seat in this small, twelve-by-sixteen-foot living room, including some folding metal chairs, was filled. The TV was on and tuned to the Sunday football game. The mourners' dress code appeared to be black jeans, black leather vests, black Harley T-shirts, and a choice of a red or blue bandana for a head covering. I felt a bit overdressed in my button-down shirt, tie, tan slacks, blue blazer, and penny loafers.

As I entered the room and stepped past the TV, a man with a beard came through the archway from the dining room and said, "Could I get you a beer?"

I smiled and said, "No, thanks." I then noticed that some of the people seated in the room were eating chips and drinking beer.

A door opened behind me in the small hallway, and a teenage girl emerged from a room and introduced herself as the daughter of the man who had died. She gave me the page she had written about her father. I opened my Bible, giving thought to starting the proceedings, and as I did so, a big, burly man with a beard and an earring got up from where he was watching the game, came over to me, and said, "You're the preacher, right?" I responded that I was, and he said, "I need to talk to you."

We took a step into the small hallway, and he said, "I was Phil's best friend, and I want you to know that Phil was saved last week before he died."

"Tell me about it," I said.

"I live in California, and I was calling Phil everyday. When he got so bad, I asked him if he would talk to a preacher, and he said he would. I go to an Assembly of God church, so I called my preacher and asked him how I could get in touch with a preacher in Phoenix to talk to my friend. He gave me a telephone number of a church here, and I called and told the pastor the situation and asked him if he would visit Phil. He said he would, and he did."

Just then the eyes of the big man began filling with tears, and as he fought them back, he said, "Phil accepted Jesus last Wednesday, and when I called him that night he told me all about it. It was the last time I talked with Phil, and I just thought you ought to know that."

I took his hand, thanked him, and said, "Man, that's beautiful, that's really beautiful. Would you like to share that as your tribute to your best friend?" He said that he would try. He returned to his seat, I turned off the TV, and the service began.

Needless to say, it was not my chosen Scriptures, my comments, or my prayers that made the service special that day. It was that man's personal and emotional sharing that was the real tribute and that provided a meaningful closure for Phil's family and friends.

Lessons for Caregivers

The dying, as well as their family and friends, can teach us many things if only we will listen to them. From Phil's memorial service

I learned again the hard lesson that "people look on the outward appearance, but God looks upon the heart" (1 Sam. 16:7). I learned how easy it is to forget the old lesson that first impressions can be misleading. Beneath the exterior of beards and beer, T-shirts and leather, there were people with grieving hearts who were uniquely qualified to celebrate the life of their deceased friend.

I was reminded again of just how special a caring friend can be. Phil's friend had a heart full of love that compelled him to do all that was within his power to share his faith with Phil before it was too late. His friendship reassured me that the quality of Andrew, the disciple of Jesus, is alive and well in our world. Each of the three times Andrew is mentioned in the Scriptures separately from the twelve disciples, he is bringing someone to Jesus.

Phil had a friend who wanted the best for him before he died, and so the friend did what he could to be sure that Phil met Jesus. Seeing the heart of such a friend and affirming his caring was a way for me to support the love they shared and an encouragement for that friend to continue being such a caring person. I never learned what Phil's friend's name was, but I'd like to think his friends called him "Andy."

chapter 5

Respecting the Hearing of the Dying

▨▨▨

*We are all teachers for one another as we face our own
dying as we live, and as we seek to comfort and understand those who, in sickness or old age, approach their
end of days.*

—Elisabeth Kübler-Ross

SUNDAY EVENING AROUND 8:30 p.m. a page came to me. I was
told that a family, through the nurse, had requested that I come as
soon as possible. I responded immediately, and in twenty minutes
I was walking into the patient's room and meeting her daughter
and granddaughter. The daughter shared with me how her mother had not been well, went into a decline, and then rallied that
morning and had a pleasant morning with them.

The granddaughter had flown in from out of state because,
when she had asked her grandmother if she should come, her
grandmother said, "If it isn't too much trouble." That was heard
as a strong "Please come." It was the granddaughter who earlier
that evening had made the suggestion to her mother that it would
be nice to get a pastor to pray with her grandmother.

The patient was a devout Catholic Christian. Her daughter and
granddaughter shared with me how throughout her life the
woman had practiced a strong faith in God. After about five minutes of listening to their celebration of the patient's wonderful life,
I turned my attention to the grandmother, who was not responsive. I cradled her hand in mine and spoke her name, introducing
myself and suggesting that she must be pleased as she listened in
on the wonderful things that had just been said about her by her

daughter and granddaughter. I speak this way with patients who are unable to respond because it is believed that hearing is possible although the eyes and lips can't respond. When speaking to non-responsive patients, I assume they hear me and are comforted by what they hear.

I suggested that we join hands, and I offered a prayer of thanks to God for the woman's life. I prayed for her spirit's soon release from the body. I then offered a prayer of thanksgiving for each of the woman's family by name and for the many ways she had blessed so many lives over the years. I prayed that as she now journeyed through the valley of the shadow of death she would know the strong hand of the Good Shepherd, who would see that she got through to the other side. When I ended my prayer, we opened our eyes. The woman released one last breath and died.

There in the silence of the room, we watched her, wondering if there would be a sudden drawing in of another breath. Finally, I broke the silence and said, "She has just passed through the valley." There were tears of amazement as both daughter and granddaughter began to reflect upon what had just happened. Both concluded that this was surely a "good death." They spoke words of thankfulness to me for my presence and prayer. "Grandma just needed to have one more prayer," said the granddaughter. "It's just one more story we can add to all of our wonderful Grandma stories."

They asked me if I'd ever had such an experience before, and I told them that this was the fifth time in six months that I'd been called to such a situation and the patient died within minutes after my prayer. I was quick to tell them I have no explanation for it, except to say that patients often seem to be in control of the timing of their deaths.

I would like to believe that a patient's sense of hearing in those final hours is more functional than her motionless body and that during that time there is comfort in having someone affirm her faith and encourage her on her journey. I can't help but wonder if the patient doesn't find that measure of strength to finally let go during a prayer. It seems as if, during our prayer, the God to whom we pray has focused full attention on welcoming the one who is coming out of the shadows.

Since this experience has happened numerous times in one of our units, the nurses have humorously given me the title of "expiration therapist." As a staff, all of us know that such an experience is a great mystery and cannot be manipulated by our actions, but we also know that we are used in mysterious ways to partner with God in accomplishing God's will.

Lessons for Caregivers

One of the great mysteries of this life is the timing of a person's death, especially the death of a person who has been in a non-responsive state for hours or days. It is believed that the timing may be related to a variety of factors, one of which is the dying person's ability to hear about and wait for an anticipated event or visit. When a death occurs shortly after a promised visitor arrives, we often conclude that the visitor's arrival is somehow associated with the timing of the death. Of course, there is no way to verify that assumption. When the patient is told who is in the room and who is on their way, he alone knows how important that information is. But the person who made that final visit doesn't need verification; he knows how important it was for him to make the visit when he did.

Caregivers often wrongfully conclude that their care-giving ceases when the patient no longer responds to them. We should instead assume that non-responsive patients can hear, and that they are still capable of exercising their will. Providing end-of-life care for a dying, non-responsive person includes knowing the person and talking to her, telling her who is present and who is on their way, and sharing with her any decisions that are being made on her behalf. We must also be mindful of what we talk about at the patient's bedside. It is not the place to discuss mortuary arrangements, the will, or who's going to get the patient's car.

As family members and caregivers wait for the death to occur, they may care for the dying person best by anticipating what it is that the dying person would appreciate, and, if at all possible, providing it for her. This is what the loving daughter and granddaughter did when they remembered that the dying woman was a religious person who valued the traditions of the church. They felt it would be appropriate for a prayer to be offered so that she could hear it, and it appears that it was the final gift that the woman needed, which in some mysterious way may have allowed her to let go.

By respecting the dying person's ability to hear, we are treating her with dignity during her dying days and providing for her through the very end of her journey.

chapter 6

Taking a Child's Grief Seriously

*We are not, after all, the "living" ministering to the
"dying." We are living persons, who will die, ministering to living persons who will die sooner.*

—*J. Donald Bane*

"LET'S SIT HERE," Joan said as she motioned for me to take the
adjoining sofa. She told the three smaller kids, "Please go into the
back room and play, and if you're nice, when we're finished I'll get
you an icy-pop." The kids hurried off.

Joan then said to her niece, "Jessica, this is the pastoral counselor from hospice I talked to earlier. He's here to answer any of
your questions."

I smiled and said hi to Jessica and asked her how old she was.

"I'm eleven."

"Eleven," I said. "That's the same age as my oldest granddaughter. What kind of questions do you have, Jessica?"

Joan spoke up and said, "Five weeks ago my mother, Jessica's
grandmother, died right here in our home. She and Jessica were
very close. Last night Jess came to spend the night with her cousins
and she slept in Me-maw's room. She cried most of the night and
was wondering if Me-maw's happy now in heaven."

Turning to Jessica, I said, "Is that important for you to know?"

With her chin down and her eyes lifted to look at me, Jessica
nodded her head and said in a quiet voice, "Yes."

"That's a good question, Jessica," I said. "I'll have to be honest
with you when I say that I don't really know the answer. What I
imagine, however, is that she is happy because she doesn't have

pain anymore, but that she may also have some sadness because she's not going to be here with you as you grow up. Does that make sense?"

Jessica lifted her head and nodded in agreement.

I then asked, "Do you often cry at night when you go to bed?" She said, "Only sometimes."

Joan said, "Her mother will tell her to 'think happy thoughts' and she'll go to sleep."

I asked Jessica, "Does that work?"

She said, "Not really. I still feel sad."

"Jessica, let me ask you something. Have you ever had a favorite toy or doll baby that you loved to play with and lost somewhere?"

The change in her face indicated that I had said something that connected with her. She said, "Yes, I lost my favorite doll baby, and never found her."

"And how did that make you feel?" I asked.

"Very sad."

"It was the same kind of feeling you have now, isn't it?"

"Uh-huh."

"Jessica, we all get sad when we lose something we value. Moms and dads and children feel sad when someone or something they have loved is no longer here. It's OK to be sad. It would be very unusual if you weren't sad that your Me-maw died. You loved her and she loved you, and you'll miss her and that's OK."

Tears began running down Jessica's cheeks. Her aunt gave her a tissue to wipe her eyes, and I said, "And it's OK to cry. You will find that as the weeks pass you will cry less, not because you don't miss her, but because you know she would want you to be happy remembering how much she loved you. Let me tell you a story and see if it helps.

"Once upon a time there was a man walking with his small daughter in the woods. As they walked they came to a place in the path where a bird had fallen from the nest and died. They stopped and the little girl asked, 'What's wrong with the bird, Daddy?'

"'The bird's dead, Tasha,' he said.

"'What's dead mean, Daddy?'

"'The bird will never move again.'

"They continued their walk, and the girl said, 'Daddy, will you die?'

"'Yes, Tasha, I will die.'

"After walking a little farther, she asked, 'Will Mommy die?'

"'Yes, Tasha, Mommy will also die.'

"Then, after a more lengthy silence, she said, 'Daddy, will I die?'

"And he said, 'Yes, Tasha, you too will die.'

"And then she asked the soul-searching question, 'But why, Daddy?'

"The father said, 'To make you precious, Tasha. Nothing that lasts forever can ever be precious.'"

I explained to Jessica how certain people and things are special because we do not always have them. It makes us appreciate them more while we have them. "Just as you appreciated your Me-maw and now you realize that you won't always have her with you," I explained. "You can still appreciate her through remembering the good times you had together. I would suggest that when you can't sleep at night and you are sad, that you think of not just something happy, but think of some happy time you and Me-maw had together."

When I finished speaking, Joan said, "Does that help, Jessica?" Jessica said that it did.

Joan walked me to the door and thanked me for coming. When I arrived at home that evening and was completing my reports for the day, I remembered that I still didn't have an ID number for the grandmother, so I called the central office where the page had originated. The person who had sent me the page searched her computers for the name and ID number, but it was nowhere to be found. We concluded that the aunt had called the wrong hospice, and I was paged before an ID number was confirmed. When I relayed this to my office case manager, her response was, "Everything happens for a reason. I think that little girl needed you today."

I agreed.

Lessons for Caregivers

Children begin to form their understanding, fears, and beliefs very early in life, and when it comes to the experiences of death and grief, adults all too often do a very poor job of providing the right direction.

Often, adults attempt to shield children from the emotional experiences related to sadness. When the goldfish dies, we get them another one. When the dog or cat dies, we replace it as soon as we can. When the favorite toy is lost, somehow another toy magically appears. However, in our effort to quiet children's tears, we are teaching them the big lie about grief: that grief is solved by substitution. Such a teaching eventually comes back to haunt us when a father, mother, or grandparent dies and we cannot say, "I'll get you another one."

Another common solution to children's sadness is offering empty words of comfort. When adults attempt to suppress a child's emotions with religious concepts and thoughtless clichés, they are only being successful at stopping the dialogue with the child. Although the concepts of heaven are important to teach, they must not be used as an escape from the emotions the child is experiencing. There's no way to convince a seven-year-old girl that "God loved Mommy so much that God wanted her in heaven." That just might communicate to her a fear of God possibly loving her "so much" that she too might die.

Children need the same thing adults need: not a replacement for what has been lost or a useless cliché, but rather someone who is willing to feel the pain of that particular loss with them. They need honest answers when it comes to understanding their emotions. It is not a bad thing to help children get in touch with their pain. To feel with them is to share with them the journey of our common humanity. It tells them that they are being taken seriously. What they feel is important, and although we cannot take away that feeling, we can share it with them. Confessing to them our own sadness, shedding with them our own tears, is a very convincing lesson that will help to shape their own spiritual journeys.

Some practical considerations: When talking with children, listen for their language and use as much of that language as you can to facilitate your communication. Using their words to identify people (in Jessica's case, her grandmother was called "Me-maw") communicates to them just who or what you are talking about. Keeping the vocabulary at the child's level is a very important way to care.

chapter 7

Faith-Based Denial

Most faith traditions encourage those who are dying to put their affairs in order and to make amends and restitution for whatever has happened in their lifetimes. These faiths believe that unresolved relationships or practical matters affect not only the way a person dies but also his course in the afterlife.

—Megory Anderson

I WAS SCANNING THROUGH the admissions material of a newly admitted patient at one of our palliative care units (a hospice facility for dying patients) when I ran across the social worker's assessment form, in which the patient was quoted as saying, "I know I'm in denial, and I don't want anyone changing my mind." I wondered about the person who would make such a statement. Can such a person be in denial if she is bold enough to verbalize it? Is the admission of denial at some level a recognition of the reality of what is being denied? My curiosity was piqued, and I decided that I must visit with this person.

The information sheet in the front of the chart told me that she was a seventy-nine-year-old woman who had breast cancer that had moved into her bones. When I entered her room, she was sitting up in her bed with her big Bible opened in her lap. I went to the bedside, introduced myself as the pastoral counselor for the unit that day, and began my conversation by noting, "I see you're into the Word early this morning."

"Yes," she replied. "I'm reading my healing verses."

I asked her how many such verses she had, and she said, "They are throughout the Bible, and they are written promising me that I'm going to be healed."

Her Bible was opened to Isaiah, so I asked, "What verse from Isaiah contains that promise for you?" She quoted for me the verse from Isaiah 53 that speaks about the suffering servant and says, "With his stripes we are healed" (53:5, KJV).

We entered into a discussion about the meaning of that verse as it relates to Jesus' death on the cross. She anticipated my difference of opinion with her interpretation and said, "You're going to tell me that the healing is meant to be from our sins, right?"

I smiled and said, "That's what it means, and yes, I was going to mention that to you."

"Well, in that case, let's not talk about it anymore."

"That's fine," I replied.

I then asked her to tell me about her disease, and she began to relate her story of discovery, treatment, and hope. As she ended her account, she said, "I have to get well before I go home."

Knowing that the word home can be misunderstood, I asked, "What do you mean by 'home'?"

She grinned at me as if I were stupid for not knowing, then said, "Home to be with the Lord!"

We talked a bit about that desire, and I challenged her with the idea that people who make the journey "home" begin it as a result of death. I reminded her that death was not a byproduct of a state of wellness or being healed. She smiled a very satisfied smile, indicating that she was content with what she believed. Looking at me, she said, "You're not going to change my mind."

I assured her that all I wanted to do was give her something to think about. Before I left, I asked her if I could pray with her, and she agreed. Back at the nurse's station, as I was writing my notes for her chart, I realized that she was very much in denial. She was a woman of great faith, and for her to admit that she might be dying would seem to contradict that faith. She died thirty-six hours later.

Lessons for Caregivers

Caregivers need to know that there are many faces of denial that a dying patient can wear, and the expression of religious faith can be one of them. Denial, although the first stage in the process of coping after hearing a terminal diagnosis, may reappear at any time. It serves as a delay tactic, giving the patient time to process information and to discover and sort through the available options. As those options are identified, the person begins to move toward understanding and acceptance, but she will most likely return to the safe harbor of denial when the facts are too hard to face.

It is helpful for caregivers to be aware of a patient's return to denial. This may be noticed in what the dying patient says. For example, the patient who speaks about her need to call the dentist and have her teeth checked, though her body is ravaged with cancer, shows the internal struggle of moving in and out of acceptance. The religious person's struggle has the added dimension of lifelong convictions that dare not be denied. The struggle for such a person is between faith convictions and medical science's diagnosis. The caregiver will hear the person using phrases such as "God can do anything" and "God answers prayer." For this patient, acceptance would be a contradiction of her religious conviction.

The dying patient with such faith convictions who is part of a faith community may also be praised by his friends for having such a "strong faith." This affirmation, which is meant to be positive, may convince the patient to seek any means possible to discover the cure God has waiting for him. As his perseverance and endurance is continually praised, he continues to be given pedestal stature. With so many people having such high expectations for him, he finds it increasingly difficult to draw the line between his personal spiritual journey and that of others. Caregivers struggle with when and how to affirm the dying patient's faith while, at the same time, attempting to help the patient move toward acceptance. The caregiver might affirm by saying, "Your faith has enabled you to endure a great deal," and then add, "but if you're not cured, then what?" This will provide the patient an opportunity to deal with denial in the presence of one who cares.

Denial is more difficult to confront when it is faith-based, but when confronted, if denial is still the patient's choice, then it must be respected. After all is said and done, we do well to remember that it is the patient's journey, not ours.

chapter 8

Faith Traditions That Care

▰▰

*Death is the one event in my life which confronts me
with the question of the meaning and purpose of life
and the significance of the future.... It is the facing of
death which forces me to deal with the question of ultimate meaning.*

—*Richard W. Doss*

THE UNIQUENESS OF BEING an on-call pastoral counselor is that
when I go out on a call, someone has specifically requested my
services. I know that there is a need and that there is the anticipation that I will in some way be able to assist in meeting that need.
However, usually I go with very little knowledge of the emotional or spiritual states of those who are grieving. I do not know what
I will find or how I will be needed, and this can be both challeng-
ing and rewarding.

It was on a Saturday afternoon when my beeper's silent alarm
quietly got my attention. I was sitting in the bleachers at a local
junior high school watching my thirteen-year-old niece play her
weekly basketball game. The beeper message was from the weekend triage secretary, requesting that I call the office concerning the
need for an urgent visit. I left a bleacher full of shouting parents
and grandparents to find a quiet space outdoors where I could use
my cell phone, and upon calling the office, I was given the name
of a thirty-year-old Navajo woman who was dying in a local
skilled nursing facility.

Thirty-five minutes later, I stepped off the elevator at the third-
floor nursing station and introduced myself to the nurse on duty.

She thanked me for coming and informed me that the young Navajo woman lay comatose, dying of alcoholism. She pointed me to the last room on the right at the end of the hall. As I walked down the hall, I could see several Native American men and women standing outside a closed door. When I reached them, I introduced myself. One of the men opened the door for me, indicating that I was to go in.

The door had to be opened slowly, because the room was jam-packed with Native American visitors. My first thought was, *How am I going to get to the bedside?* But, when one woman read my nametag, she said something in her native tongue, and the people moved quietly to provide me access to the room.

I eased my way to the foot of the bed, noticing an elderly Navajo woman sitting on a chair at the head of the bed. The side rails were down, and she was gently stroking the long, coal-black hair of the dying woman. She was singing a Christian hymn in their native language, and some others in the room were doing their best through their tears to sing along. I immediately recognized the tune as "What a Friend We Have in Jesus." The woman leading the singing had an expression of confidence and acceptance as she sang. Those around me sang and spoke the words as if claiming an old truth for the first time: "All our sins and griefs to bear." I did not know the language, but I was certain of the truth.

When the song ended, the elderly woman at the bedside talked to the comatose woman. She treated the patient as though she could hear all that was going on, because, as earlier noted, a person in such a state is often able to hear although she cannot respond. The woman told the patient who was there in the room; she named names and told the patient how much they loved her.

A younger woman was on the opposite side of the bed, holding the patient's hand, crying, and stroking her arm. Someone behind me said in my ear, "That's her sister." Then the elderly woman began another song, this time in English, but it wasn't one I knew, so I listened. The words spoke of hope and trust in a God who cares for us beyond this earthly life.

Several other hymns were sung in English, and I joined in on the ones I knew. Then there was a pause, and an older Navajo man in a plaid work shirt with a gray pigtail sticking out from under a black cap began praying in English. It was a beautiful prayer of thanksgiving and blessing upon the one who was dying and those who were gathered there. He thanked God for the patient's love and her trust in Jesus, and with quiet strength he committed her to God's eternal care and keeping.

After the prayer, the old woman began singing "In the Sweet Bye and Bye," and as I sang I kept my eyes on the dying woman. (I have learned to watch a patient's breathing when I can't hear it.) When we finished the last stanza of the hymn, I noticed that the patient had stopped breathing. I motioned to the person closest to the door to get the nurse.

The nurse came and checked the patient's vital signs, then reported that the woman had died. That moment is such a final one, no matter how long a person has been ill. It is a moment of release. There were tears and crying, and as a benediction upon her life and on the Christian hope about which we had been singing, I reassured them all that the words of their last hymn may have given her the assurance that she needed in order to let go. I repeated the words "In the sweet bye and bye we *will* meet on that beautiful shore." I offered a final blessing on all who shared that special moment and then returned to the nursing station and wrote my brief report in the patient's chart.

I rode the elevator back down to the lobby and walked out to my car, realizing how privileged I had been to gather in a room with persons of different cultural traditions and yet feel the power of the Spirit that comforted and consoled a grieving community. I had been able to help, not by offering my own thoughts or advice, but by participating in what the others knew to be best for the dying woman.

Lessons for Caregivers

The resources of comfort and hope do not always need to come from a professional or an assigned caregiver; they can just as easily come from those who are experiencing grief and sorrow over a loved one's impending death. Being sensitive to the resources that are present and helpful is an important skill for a caregiver to develop.

The caring community that supported the dying Navajo woman gave me a new appreciation for how one's spiritual journey may be shaped by one's community. Among Native Americans there are strong religious traditions that are taught and carried out so that each member of the community will be able to see and understand who they are and how they relate to themselves and to others. Christian hymns committed to memory enabled those who gathered at the dying woman's bedside to sing words that reaffirmed the promises of God. The promises that had shaped each individual in his or her personal spiritual journey revealed who they were as children of God and also how they were related as people bonded together by more than tribal name or common ancestors.

Anyone who dies surrounded by those who love her and celebrate with her the beliefs they all hold dear, as this Navajo woman did, has received an immeasurable gift. Caregivers who are sensitive to this important dynamic will be able to affirm the community and traditions of families and friends by offering a supportive presence without having to be in control.

chapter 9

Faith, Unanswered Prayer, and God's Will

We don't "get over" the deepest pains of life, nor should we. "Are you over it?" is a question that cannot be asked by someone who has been through "it," whatever "it" is. It is an anxious question, an asking for reassurance that cannot be given.

—Madeleine L'Engle

TAMMY WAS FORTY-TWO years old and dying of cancer in the liver and pancreas. Her husband, Michael, and their teenage daughter were at her bedside around the clock in one of our palliative care units. The nursing staff indicated to me that they thought the husband would appreciate a visit, since his wife had not been responsive for the last two days. They also indicated that he was very much in denial of the late stage of her disease.

I entered the room and was warmly received by Michael, who was holding his wife's hand. The jaundiced skin on her face was a certain indication of the rapid spread of the disease. After I had introduced myself, Michael quickly volunteered that he was a "born-again" Christian who was a practicing Catholic. His conversation was very positive as he shared with me the journey of his wife's illness. As I listened to him, I understood what the staff meant when they said that he was in denial. He said to me, with conviction and confidence, "My wife is going to walk out of this unit. I believe God is going to heal her."

I affirmed that it would be a wonderful miracle, but then I asked, "What if God doesn't permit that miracle to happen? Have you thought of that?"

Michael nodded his head, but he quickly replied, "But God's going to do it. I've been praying that this would be God's will for a long time, and I've even asked God for a sign of a white dove."

He continued to tell me how hopeful he was, and I continued to try to interject the reality of his wife's disease without robbing him of his great faith. After praying with Michael, each of us holding a hand of his wife, I left.

After this encounter, I had mixed feelings. I knew the reality of Tammy's disease, and yet I believed the Scriptures that Michael had quoted to me about "faith that can move mountains" (Matt. 17:20). I marveled at his boldness to ask God for a sign of a white dove. It was so specific. Was he perhaps being specific so that he could be more accepting when she died without his receiving the sign?

Since I am on call only on weekends and Tammy was very ill, I felt that it would be unlikely that I would see Michael again. But the following Sunday when I arrived at the unit, before I could even check the board to see the names of the patients, one of the nurses asked me if I had heard about Michael. I told her I hadn't, and she told me that the day before, as he was sitting at his wife's bedside, a white dove flew down and perched on the back of the bench outside the window. I'm sure my mouth dropped open and my eyes widened with great interest. The nurse went on to tell me how the dove had sat there for the longest time, even when children walked by and someone went out to fill the bird feeder. It just quietly stayed there, and when it flew away, no one saw it leave. She added that prior to that day none of the nurses ever remembered seeing a white dove in that courtyard by that feeder.

I went to Tammy's room, and when I entered, I was warmly greeted by Michael and his teenage daughter, Melissa. I could see by his smile that Michael was eager to share his experience with me, and he did. He sincerely believed that the sign was from God and that his wife was going to be healed. I again affirmed how wonderful that would be, but I was careful to recognize the progress of the disease.

As we talked, I asked Michael, "What if she dies but you've seen the white dove?"

He thought for a moment, shaking his head from side to side without saying a word. Finally, he said, "I've always prayed that she would be healed, but as I told you last week, I also always pray, 'Thy will be done.' I know that whatever happens, it will be God's will." The three of us stood by the bedside and shared a closing prayer together.

When I arrived at the unit the following weekend, Tammy had died. I have unfinished thoughts about how Michael and his daughter were able to accept Tammy's death. I cannot help but wonder about the white dove and what it meant. Was it an answer to Michael's prayer for healing—not the healing of a physical body, but of that wholeness that comes when our very beings are released from earthly pain and suffering? Since the white dove is the symbol of our hospice organization, could it have been an affirmation that bringing Tammy into our hospice care was exactly the right decision?

One thing I'm sure of is this: Every time Michael and Melissa see a white dove, it brings a smile to their lips and joy to their hearts. I believe it reminds them that, however their prayers were answered, God was with them.

Lessons for Caregivers

Michael's strong faith was expressed in his bold request for a specific sign that his wife would be healed. It was an expression of his personal struggle with end-of-life issues as they related to his faith. He believed both in "the will of God" and in following the biblical teaching to be specific in praying: "For everyone who asks receives, and everyone who searches finds, and for everyone who knocks, the door will be opened" (Luke 11:10). Michael wasn't willing to accept the diagnosis of death, but he was willing to accept the will of God.

Caregivers need to understand Michael's kind of faith-based confidence as having less to do with denial and more to do with preparation for living in the future. Accepting the will of God is preparation for living in the future when there is no miracle. A supportive caregiver will hear the hope of healing and will pray with the patient and family to that end, all the while knowing that the family has not based their hope on a single text, but on the wider teaching of Scripture. The family very likely understands that God's will may not be their own. This does not mean they cannot pray in faith. Such prayer is like Jacob's wrestling with the angel on the ladder from heaven (Gen. 32:24-29). It is prayer that will not let go unless a blessing is also provided. Sometimes—indeed often—the prayer is not answered in the way we would like. But this does not diminish the faith of the Christian whose hope is shaped by a confidence in the will of God.

chapter 10

When God Appears to Someone

[Death] has two sides, as the sea has two shores. We see only one, the less important one: the common departure from the familiar place, not the various arrivals at the new one...yet ships arrive at different ports; neither their existence nor their uniqueness is extinguished.

—*Peter J. Kreeft*

I'VE NOT HAD MANY "normal" people tell me that God has appeared to them. It's not uncommon for patients with mental illnesses to claim such an epiphany, and I've had plenty of Alzheimer's patients tell me bizarre stories that would baffle any rational mind. But the first time I ever had anyone claim to have seen God, it was a person who did not have a mental illness. Eldon, whom I met during my Clinical Pastoral Education (CPE) as a seminarian at the Danvers State Mental Hospital in Massachusetts, had been admitted to one of our palliative care units because of congestive heart failure. When I walked into his room he was sitting up on the edge of his bed in a hunter green pair of pajamas. He had just finished his noon meal and was pushing the tray and bedside table away from his bed.

I offered him my hand and told him my name. He leaned closer to see the ID badge that hung beneath the buttons on my shirt. He looked up at me and said, "Bill, it's nice to meetcha."

Since my visit was the first that any of our pastoral counselors had made to Eldon, I began by telling him a bit about our services. I mentioned how important the nursing care is for providing the body comfort from pain. I went on to explain that the pastoral counselors are present to assist patients with any matters that may be spiritual. I told him that we are available twenty-four hours a day, seven days a week, and that although he might not see us in the unit, we could be reached by any of the nursing staff.

"Thank you," he said. "That sounds like a good deal."

There was a lull in the conversation, and Eldon reached for his water cup and took a sip. As he did, I noticed a ring on his finger that was made of jade with an inlaid gold cross. Thinking that commenting on the ring would give me an opportunity to explore Eldon's personal faith, I ventured, "Eldon, that's a very unusual ring."

"Well, it's a very special ring, and if you'd like to know the story behind it, I'd be glad to tell you."

I told him that I was eager to hear it. Eldon fondled the ring, turning it on his finger. Then, he began, "One night I had to get up to go pee. It was about three in the morning. When I came back and got into bed I lay there for a moment, and when I turned on my right side, I realized someone was in the room. It was God, and he said, 'Don't worry or be afraid about the future. Trust me; I'll take care of you.'"

He paused for a moment, and then with a smile on his face said, "You may think I'm wacko, but it happened." Then he continued, "I lay back on the pillow next to my wife, who was sleeping, and I fell back to sleep. When I thought about it the next morning, I concluded that it had been a dream.

"It must have been two or three weeks later that it happened again. This time I was going to bed around 1 a.m. My wife was always in bed earlier than me. She was sound asleep. I was sitting on the edge of my bed, taking my socks off, and I had that same feeling. In the darkness of the room, without lifting my eyes from my socks on the floor, I knew God was standing there again. He said the same thing: 'Don't worry or be afraid about the future. Trust me; I'll take care of you.' Since I hadn't been asleep yet, I knew I wasn't dreaming. To be honest, I was scared.

"The next day, I thought some more about it, but after a couple of days I decided it wasn't something I wanted to tell anyone. You know what they'd think. I decided to just forget about it, and I did until about a month later when he showed up again in my bedroom with the same message.

"I woke up at about 5:30 the next morning, got up, dressed, and went down to my friend's jewelry store. I've always had a key because I've worked with him making different kinds of jewelry. I picked out some stones and began making a ring, but the first three kinds of stones kept breaking on me until I settled on this jade. I cut it and polished it and then shaped the gold cross and soldered it to the base and set the four pieces of jade around it. I ground it smooth and polished it and put it on my finger. That was six years ago, and I wouldn't take a million dollars for it."

I was silent as I watched Eldon turn the ring around his finger and examine it. Then he smiled at me and said, "You can believe it or not. It doesn't matter to me, 'cause what others believe about it can't change what I know."

I told Eldon that I believed him and asked, "Since you've made the ring, has God appeared to you anymore?"

He shook his head, and said, "No, but he's been with me. My wife died a couple of years ago, and it was then that I recalled the words he told me, 'Don't worry or be afraid about the future,' so I didn't worry and I wasn't afraid."

"Does that mean that you have that same confidence now that you've been told you probably have less than six months to live?" I asked.

"Exactly. I'm not the least bit worried, and I'm not at all afraid to die."

Before I left, we shared a prayer of thanksgiving together. I offered thanks for God's faithfulness in caring for Eldon and giving him the confidence to face the uncertainties of life without worry or fear.

Lessons for Caregivers

It only takes the simple recognition of something that is important to a dying person to give him permission to tell his story. Because I noticed Eldon's ring and asked about it, he was able to share with me an experience that had changed his life. Spiritual formation occurs through a variety of religious experiences. Most often we credit the church and devout parents as the conduits through which information and inspiration flow, but Eldon's experience was different. It breaks through our usual assumptions that connect religious faith to traditional, organized religion. Eldon did not even confess to being a religious man or to being associated with any organized church. And it didn't matter to him if anyone else believed his story, because another person's response was not going to change an experience that he highly valued.

Epiphanies such as Eldon experienced are not the typical path taken on a spiritual journey. Not too many caregivers are qualified to sit with someone like him and respond with a story of their own in validation of his. I know I wasn't, but I could affirm that such an experience doesn't take validation from someone else in order for it to be important. After all, clergy and some laypersons have had experiences of being "called" to a particular form of Christian ministry, and no amount of suspicion or skepticism on the part of others can rob the person who was "called" of what he knows he has experienced.

The caregiver who has this broader awareness of a God who "works in mysterious ways" will be more attuned to the unique stories the dying share with them.

chapter 11

A Spiritually Disturbed Christian

One way to discover the dying person's needs is to encourage memory work and life review. It may be helpful for someone close to the dying person to listen to the pain and explore the feelings about this unwanted journey into death.

—Alice Parsons Zulli and O. Duane Weeks

IT WAS EARLY FRIDAY evening when an admitting nurse paged me to request that I visit with a new patient. Barbara was sixty-five years old and suffering from lung and heart disease. She lived alone and had indicated that there were some serious spiritual and emotional issues she needed to talk about.

I arrived at the independent living facility where she was staying and was given directions to her apartment. A note on the door said, "Door's open, come in." I knocked and entered, identified myself, and was welcomed to sit in a chair by the folding snack tray near where the patient was sitting in her recliner. After I sat down, Barbara said, "Tell me what it is you do."

I told her briefly about my role as a pastoral counselor with Hospice of the Valley. She then said, "I'm profoundly spiritually disturbed." She paused, and I asked if she would say more about the issues that disturbed her.

She then began to tell me her story. She went back to over four years ago when she was in the hospital for surgery. She said, "I had an experience of neither being here in this world nor in the hereafter. It was a gray area, and I was aware of the Spirit of God being present but not active. I had a sensation of pain in my rib, as if it were being pierced with a sword. My rib has bothered me over the years. I broke it at a very early age. This place was not a pleasant place to be. I was aware of my suffering and realized that it was nothing compared to what Christ went through on the cross. The pain in my rib gave the feeling of the spear that went into the side of Christ, and I felt so terrible that he had to suffer so. The Spirit was there with me but did nothing to relieve my pain, and I have lived with this, not being able to understand it. I've not understood why the Spirit did nothing to help me in that experience. I have not had anyone to share this with, and I am hoping you can help me."

"Just how is it you feel that I can help you with this?" I asked.

"Well," she said, "I was hoping you could help me make some sense out of it, especially why the Spirit did nothing to help me."

"I can't begin to say that I know what the experience means for you," I said, "but I can share with you my thoughts about it."

She smiled and said, "Please do."

I told her that what she had experienced sounded very much like what Christ went through on the cross, as she had indicated. I reminded her that few of us ever experience suffering to the degree that makes us appreciate the extent of Christ's suffering for us, and it sounded to me like she had done so. She had felt not only the physical pain in her side, but the emotional abandonment that Christ felt. She knew that the Spirit was present in the situation, but he was not acting on her behalf. I reminded her that Christ knew that same Spirit and spoke to the Spirit when he cried, "My God! My God! Why have you forsaken me?" Her anguish over the silence of God identified with the anguish of Christ. I paused and asked, "Is any of this making sense to you?"

She nodded her head in agreement, as tears filled her eyes. "But why did he have to suffer so much?" she asked.

I replied, "I only know what the Scriptures teach: 'Without the shedding of blood there is no forgiveness of sins' (Hebrews 9:22).

The Lamb of God shed his blood so that our sins would be forgiven. Now as soon as I say that, I must be honest with you and say that I don't really know the answer to your 'why' either. For me the awareness of such mysteries is where my faith is exercised. Faith is where we must take our unanswered questions."

She looked up, smiling, and said, "Thank you very much. That helps me more than you'll ever know."

We prayed together, and when I finished, she offered her own prayer expressing her gratefulness to God for his forgiveness and love. I left Barbara knowing she had become more accepting and peaceful. I realized it was not so much from what I said, but from her being able to share her struggle with someone who would listen.

Lessons for Caregivers

When a dying patient confesses to being "profoundly spiritually disturbed," it gets your attention. A "near-death" experience (NDE) had left Barbara with questions about what she had felt during the experience and what she continued to feel ever since. She wanted to understand that past experience before she died. Many people believe that they have returned from such an experience. The phenomenon of NDEs has grown since Raymond Moody's book *Life after Life* was published in 1975.

Most people who return from such an experience have a new awareness of their spiritual selves, as well as a new resolve to live a more full and meaningful life. For some, like Barbara, that means coming to terms with the feelings that were indelibly imprinted on their memories during the experience. Going to the edge of life itself increased Barbara's determination to be prepared when she returned to that edge at a later point in life. Those intervening four years had a profound influence upon her as she wrestled with her unanswered questions.

When caregivers listen to people tell their stories, it is important that they listen for the unresolved questions that may simply need to be talked out. When the dying are convinced that their care-givers are willing to listen to them, even though the caregivers might not have any answers, they discover that there is someone who cares to share the journey with them.

Barbara's eagerness to pray about her situation indicates that she recognized the source of true caring—God. Her prayer of gratitude reflected a contentment and peace that showed that she was no longer "profoundly spiritually disturbed."

chapter 12

Emotional and Spiritual Pain Levels

A person who fears death does not usually bring comfort to the grieved…. But comfort comes from those who have coped with the issues of life and death in their own souls and offer to the other the strength they have found.

—*Gladys M. Hunt*

RICK WAS THIRTY-FOUR years old and had been battling brain cancer for two years. During that time he was living out of the country and married a woman who had a nine-year-old child. After several rounds of chemotherapy, Rick faced the realization that there was nothing more anyone could do for him. Living far from home, he faced the choice of staying where he was or moving back to live with his family in Arizona. He returned for a visit, along with his wife and her child, and they decided to stay. His mother agreed to move out of her home and stay with her sister so that Rick and his family could have their space.

When I first met Rick he had been in the hospice for about two weeks and in one of our care units for four days. My pager went off at 5:45 p.m. on a Friday evening. The nurse on duty wanted to know if I was available to go to the unit soon. I told her I would be there in about forty minutes.

When I arrived, she thanked me for coming and shared that they were having difficulty controlling Rick's pain and that it wouldn't be until Monday when they could move him to another unit where a nearby physician would be able to administer and monitor a new form of pain control for him. The nurse was concerned that Rick would want to go home over the weekend and didn't think that would be best for him. She also said, "He has some issues that he needs to talk about with someone. Maybe he'll talk with you."

When I walked into the room, Rick was standing at the sink washing his face and rinsing out his mouth. There was a woman talking on the telephone whom I assumed to be his mother, since the nurse had said that Rick's mother was in the room with him. As the woman hung up the telephone, the nurse entered the room with a can of Coke. She said to Rick, "I've brought you some Coke and also someone I'd like you to meet."

Rick finished combing his hair, turned, and said, "I think I need to get back into bed." He walked past me and very carefully lowered himself to a sitting position on the edge of the bed. The nurse put the Coke on the table, and Rick stood up very slowly and stuck out his hand.

After we introduced ourselves, Rick sat down again on the bed, the nurse excused herself, and I took a chair beside the bed. Rick's mother introduced herself and came over to sit in the other available chair. She thanked me for coming and said to Rick, "Maybe Bill could tell us a little about himself."

I shared a bit about my years of pastoral experience and my role as a weekend on-call pastoral counselor. After a brief pause, I added, "Why don't you tell me about yourselves?"

Rick's mother, looking at Rick, said, "Do you want me to tell Bill what's been happening?"

Rick nodded his head and said, "Sure, go ahead."

She said, "If I say anything you don't want me to say, you just say, 'Don't go there, Mother.'" She began by telling me about the progress and treatment of Rick's cancer and how the physical pain was pretty severe at times. She told me how two years ago Rick had married a young mother with a child and how there had been a great deal of stress in the relationship due to the child losing her mother's full attention. She spoke of how the stress had not been good for Rick, and how his wife had accused him of being a "Mommy's boy." Rick's mother felt trapped. She wanted to care for her son, with whom she had a close relationship, and now that he was terminally ill she wanted to do whatever he requested.

That week, Rick had asked that his wife give him some warning when she was going to bring her daughter along to the hospice because he needed to prepare himself for the visit. She took offense at that, and this caused him great anxiety. Rick and his mother both shared a variety of examples illustrating how fragile the relationship was, and Rick confessed that it caused him a lot of pain.

After talking for about forty minutes, Rick's mother asked him if he'd like to talk to me alone. He said he would, so she excused herself, left the room, and closed the door. We shared a few moments of silence, and then I asked, "What have you been thinking about, Rick, that you would like to share with me?"

He then began to speak about his faith, about how he had really messed up in life by getting into drugs and three bad marriages, and how he should be doing more for the Lord. He said, "I just can't concentrate lately when I try to read the Bible, and I know I should be reading it more. I feel like the sluggard in Proverbs—you know, like the ant."

I responded, "Is someone telling you that you should be reading it more?"

"Well, yeah," he said. "My wife."

I said, "Rick, you're not in the best physical shape to be concentrating on reading material, are you?'

He looked at me, smiled, and said, "You got that right."

I asked, "Don't you think God knows that?"

He nodded his head, signifying agreement, then said, "But I've been so bad!"

"And what have you done about that?" I asked.

"I've confessed it, and God's forgiven me, but I just can't forget it."

"Rick, just because God forgives us doesn't mean that God expects us to forget it. Not forgetting helps keep us from repeating the mistake."

He looked up, took a drink of his Coke, and said, "I suppose you're right, but I have this feeling that I should do more."

"That's not a bad feeling, Rick, because in feeling that you can begin to understand God's wonderful grace. Our feeling of wanting to do more is our way of wishing we could do something to become more worthy so that God would be more likely to accept us."

"I know, I know," he replied. "But I've really messed up."

After a pause I said, "Well, let me suggest that we share a prayer together, and then I'll return tomorrow and we'll continue our conversation." I could see that he was getting tired and even dozing a little during our conversation.

He said, "That sounds good! I'd like that."

I held Rick's hand and prayed that he would have courage and strength to face his physical, emotional, and spiritual pain.

As I left the room that night, I was able to appreciate anew the variety of pain that dying patients experience. It is not hard to notice and care for the physical pain that is brought on by disease, but sometimes we fail to see the deeper pain that is experienced in the relationships of family members who are confronting their grief but who are not all "on the same page." When we miss seeing this, we may also miss seeing the spiritual pain that emerges out of the dying person's struggle to deal with his beliefs and the fears that arise from unanswerable questions of faith.

I saw Rick the next day, and he expressed some fear that Jesus was going to come down and he was going to "miss the train." I asked him what train he meant, and he said, "The train to heaven." I asked him if he knew what the name of that train was, and he said, "No, do you?"

I said, "I'd like to think it is the Amazing Grace Express, because everyone riding that train has had a ticket paid for, and you, Rick, can be sure there's a seat reservation in your name."

He smiled and said, "Yeah, I like that."

I saw Rick twice in the next ten days before he died. I conducted the funeral service and shared with those in attendance Rick's acceptance of God's grace. That grace did not free him from his physical pain, but it did ease his emotional and spiritual pain and permit him to die in peace.

Lessons for Caregivers

Pain is something we all know, and we normally speak of it in terms of our physical bodies. Medical science today has a variety of ways to offer quick relief from physical pain. The medical personnel who care for the dying will ask where the pain is on a scale of one to ten and then provide the appropriate medication to bring relief. Families are easily content if their loved one is not "suffering" but is kept comfortable. Thus it is easy for a caregiver to conclude that a person who has been given the proper medicine is "pain-free."

Caregivers, however, must recognize that pain exists not only in the physical but in the emotional and spiritual realms as well. Rick's physical pain was severe, but his emotional and spiritual pain was just as real, and for that no amount of morphine could help him. He needed a caregiver who was able to help identify the source of the emotional and spiritual pain and offer some relief. Caring for a dying person includes seeing beyond the physical symptoms of pain management in an effort to discover those relationships in which emotional and spiritual pain exist and, then, offering some hope. Such a caregiver must often be outside of the family, because family members may themselves be contributing to the pain.

The unpacking of Rick's emotional and spiritual pain proceeded at his pace, and I had to be aware of how much of that painful sharing he was able to bear and how much stress it was causing him. The caregiver needs to assess how much is helpful and how much ought to be left for another time. A good caregiver will make that call and then make a promise to return so that the conversation can be continued at another time. This ensures that the patient knows that the caregiver is aware of the patient's discomfort, and it also provides the patient with the hope of seeing the caregiver again.

The preliminary conversation that I had with Rick and his mother is also a reminder that, as caregivers, we must establish some level of trust with a patient before we are invited to share his painful journey. When Rick's mother volunteered to leave the room, she was telling me that trust had been established and it was time to proceed. It is important that the caregiver be sensitive to the signals of those being cared for, to know when that level of trust has been reached.

chapter 13

The Fear of Grieving Alone

You may feel that God is singling you out for tragedy. How many living saints do you know? ... Loss has nothing to do with rewards and punishment. You and your loved one are not being disciplined by God. God doesn't consult a divine computer to find out who is most deserving or who can handle it best.

—Earl A. Grollman

IT WAS A SUNDAY EVENING, and I had stayed up late watching a movie on television. I had been in bed for about twenty minutes when, at 12:15 a.m., my beeper went off and I awakened to my wife shaking me and saying, "I think someone needs you." I telephoned the palliative care unit and was told that Bonnie, a fifteen-year-old mother, was sitting alone with her six-month-old baby, who was not expected to live through the night. The young mother did not want the baby to die while she was alone and had requested a pastoral counselor.

When I arrived, Bonnie was curled up in bed, cuddling her baby, who was attached to an oxygen machine by a tube taped to her nose. The nurse introduced me to Bonnie, and I sat on the edge of the bed. I learned that the young mother was very much alone, with no family support. The baby's father had never been in the picture during the six months of the baby's life, which had been spent mostly in and out of hospitals dealing with the complications of the baby's health.

The nurse came back into the room and asked Bonnie if she would like to go outside with me to talk while the nurse held the baby. Bonnie hesitated, then said, "OK, but call me if there's any change."

We stepped outside and sat in some patio chairs. Bonnie lit up a cigarette. She was quick to tell me that she didn't understand why this was happening, because during her pregnancy she had been so careful not to smoke or drink. She told me of how she had waited for her baby's birth with some simple hopes and dreams. I asked what those hopes were, and she said, "I just wanted her to be healthy so I could take her to the park and push her in her carriage."

After about fifteen minutes, the nurse returned and said, "You'd better come back in now." We went back inside, and Bonnie sat in a recliner with the baby on her chest. I knelt beside the chair and stroked the baby's hair while Bonnie held her close. Soon Bonnie had dozed off and the baby's breathing became very quiet. I pulled up a chair near them and waited.

As I waited, I watched the baby's small chest move with each breath. The baby, although in a comatose condition, would at times appear restless and at other times motionless. After about an hour, Bonnie awoke, stiff from her position in the recliner. I suggested that she and the baby return to the bed, and they did, soon falling asleep again.

I returned to my watching and waiting. I had to stand near the bed because of the dim light in the room. Over the next five hours as I stood there, Bonnie awoke two times and saw me standing there and then went back to sleep. She knew that she was not alone, that someone was with her and her baby.

That morning after 8:00 a.m. another pastoral counselor arrived to relieve me. Bonnie was still sleeping as I slipped out of the room and into the morning sun. On my drive home I thought of the nights I had waited not for a baby to die but for a baby to be born. I remembered nights spent waiting to become a father and a grandfather as my wife and daughter went through the pain of childbirth. Waiting for babies to be born is normal; waiting for them to die is not.

Bonnie's baby lived for only another week. The young mother, who knew nothing would change the circumstances of her baby's condition, had asked only for what any of us would desire: not to have to wait alone.

Lessons for Caregivers

There is no more difficult grief than that of a parent when a child dies. The age of the child does not matter. When an adult child dies before his parents, the parents know it shouldn't happen that way. It is even more difficult when a baby is given no chance of growing to adulthood. Parents of such children experience a range of emotions for which they are unprepared. Bonnie was grieving the loss of her daughter, who would never see her seven-month birthday. Bonnie's youthful inexperience with life and her lack of family support did not prepare her to deal with the shattering news that her baby was going to die.

Bonnie's grief was defined not by the number of days or months the baby had lived, but by the future days and months that she would not live. Bonnie was not even grieving that she would not see the child graduate from high school and college, but only that Bonnie would never be able to push her baby in a carriage in the park.

Bonnie's circumstances compounded her grief. Without the father of the baby or her parents' support, she felt very alone. As she struggled with her own past, she was quick to excuse herself from having done anything during her pregnancy that might have caused the baby's illness. She just wanted to know why the baby was dying, as if knowing would in some way make it more acceptable.

Just the title "caregiver" implies that someone gives something to someone else and in the giving has provided that person with a source of help. It is an active word, and because of this, caregivers are easily conditioned to define their role as an activity. Care-giving, as earlier noted, is something we do.

However, caregivers should be warned that there are times

when they will feel that they have done very little and will maybe even feel guilty for not having spoken many words. At such a time it is good to remember that words are often inadequate and out of place when providing care for those who are grieving. There are times when we feel a need to speak up, to do something, and end up feeling like we've said the wrong thing. We must honor the silence and understand that our presence alone does the speaking for us. Clergy and laypersons must be convinced that it is not always what we say with words that makes a difference but what we share in our presence.

Bonnie was not seeking someone with answers or solutions, only someone who would be with her so that she would not be alone when her baby died. I will be honest with you: This kind of caring is more difficult than any other. This kind of care-giving demands the expenditure of emotional energy that can physically tire and drain a person more than a day's hard labor. Such is the calling of the caregiver.

chapter 14

Honor the Care Receiver's Faith

*It is the LORD who goes before you. He will be with
you; he will not fail you or forsake you. Do not fear or
be dismayed.*

—*Deuteronomy 31:8, NRSV*

IT WAS SATURDAY EVENING when my pager contact informed me
of a need at one of our palliative care units. When I heard the
name of the patient, I immediately suspected that he might be Jewish. When I arrived at the patient's room, I found it to be filled
with family members. The young men were wearing yarmulkes
(skullcaps). A woman with gray hair who was standing by the bed
looked at me as I entered the room; I concluded that she was the
wife of the dying man. I introduced myself to her, and she said,
"Pastor, thank you for coming. Jacob is not going to make it, and
we need you to be here."

Not that there was much doubt, but I confirmed with them that
they were Jewish and then asked if it would be helpful if I contacted a Rabbi for them. The woman smiled and said, "No, our
God is your God, and he hears our prayers."

I affirmed her statement and, since Jacob was not responding, I
asked her if he had the assurance of God's love and care in these
dying days. She smiled again and said, "Oh, yes, he knew."

I then was introduced to every person in the room, and the
woman directed a grandson to get me a chair so that I could sit
with her by the bed. I sat down, and I invited the people in the
room to tell me about Jacob as they knew him. Different ones
spoke up, telling me about their relationship with him and sharing

some little remembrance of how special he was to them. There was laughter as they remembered things that had happened or lessons they had learned.

An hour passed so quickly, and when the time was appropriate, I stood and told them how special it was for Jacob and his wife to have such a loving family present at such a time. I encouraged them to keep telling their stories and to tell Jacob how much he meant to them. I usually conclude my visits with a prayer, and I wanted to be sensitive to how I, a Baptist, could best minister to this Jewish family, so I asked them if I could leave them with a prayer and a blessing from the Old Testament.

They agreed this would be very good, so I read to them the twenty-third Psalm, offered a prayer, and then blessed them with the benediction from Deuteronomy 31:8: "It is the LORD who goes before you. He will be with you; he will not fail you or forsake you. Do not fear or be dismayed."

As I rode the elevator to the lobby, I was very much aware that I had just experienced a special moment unlike any I had ever experienced before. I was able to facilitate a meaningful closure with people whose religious experiences were in some ways similar and yet very different from mine. It was affirming to know that being sensitive to the belief system that has given people hope through the years makes it possible to connect with them in a very special way.

Lessons for Caregivers

Caregivers will discover that those people who have had a meaningful faith experience in life are most often the best prepared to accept death. The teaching and inspiration by which they have lived provides them with an inner confidence and trust at the time of death. They have lived a lifetime of values and beliefs that have provided them with assurance and the knowledge of God.

Jacob and his family shared such a faith experience. Caregivers who participate in this kind of situation must recognize that their first priority is to invite the family to examine their beliefs and then to take the opportunity to affirm those beliefs as the family's needed hope and support. The caregiver needs to remember that he is not there to change the family's beliefs if they differ from his own. Regardless of the label they put on their meaningful religious experiences, when people are able to articulate those beliefs with confidence and trust in a God who loves them, the caregiver should affirm them by seeking a common ground where their faith traditions intersect. In my situation, my faith and the faith of the Jewish family was nurtured in the common ground of the Old Testament. From the Scriptures we both knew and valued, we were able to hear the Word of God for us in that moment.

I would remind all caregivers that what we do and say should be for the good of the dying patient and his family, and the attitude we bring to such a moment will shape the quality of our caring. It is an attitude that consciously remembers that whatever we do and say, it must be all about the mourning family and *their* personal faith values, not about us and our beliefs.

chapter 15

Forgiveness Minimizes the Regrets

You may ask: "Dear God, why me? Why us?" ...
Know this: No one has a complete understanding of
why good people go through such tortuous times. No
philosopher or theologian has a cosmic computer to plug
into this unknown secret formula.

—*Earl A. Grollman*

I FIRST MET LOIS on my routine rounds one Saturday morning. She was an eighty-two-year-old woman who had survived a stroke several years ago and now faced a terminal illness. I discovered quickly that she was a woman of faith who had the support of her church. There was something that clicked between us in those few minutes we spent together. Before leaving the unit that morning, I stopped by her room to say good-bye to the charge nurse who was working with Lois behind the privacy curtain. When she heard me, Lois said in her stammering, stroke-hindered voice, "Good-bye, Bill."

I replied, "Good-bye, Lois."

The next time I appeared in the unit, I was met by a social worker who was talking with a young lady, and when I approached, the worker said to the young lady, "This is Bill." It was as though they had been talking about me, and I soon discovered that indeed they had been.

The young woman, Sarah, was Lois's daughter, and she had been asking who Bill was, as her mother had asked for me on several occasions. I spoke briefly with the daughter, and then we went in together to visit with Lois.

I gathered from the conversation we had that there was a strained relationship with another daughter, who hadn't seen her mother in over four years. It wasn't something they were eager to talk about at that time.

Over the next two weeks I visited Lois each time I was in the unit. Her charts indicated that she was unhappy and even angry at times with different staff members. As a staff we discussed this, and the social worker asked me if, since Lois thought so much of me, I would try to find out what was troubling her. I said I would and went right to Lois's room.

As we talked, I could see in Lois's eyes a troubled look and a heavy brow that showed signs of fear. I confronted her with what I'd noticed by saying, "Lois, are you afraid of something?"

"Yes," came the reply.

"Are you afraid of dying?" I asked.

She said, "No."

I then asked, "Are you afraid you might die before you can do something? Is there something that you are afraid will not get done before you die?"

And she said, "Yes."

As I looked into her eyes, in which small pools of tears were beginning to form, I asked, "Would you tell me what it is that you are afraid won't get done?"

"My daughters won't believe that I'm sorry for how I've treated them."

I then listened as Lois told me how she had not been a good mother, had abused her daughters verbally, and at times had treated them very badly. She had often told them she was sorry, but she then did it again, so that after several times of expressing her remorse she just returned to her old ways. She knew it was why her other daughter had refused to see her anymore. But neither did she feel that the daughter, Sarah, who had been so dutifully caring for her, had accepted her pleas for forgiveness either.

I prayed with Lois and promised her that I would do what I could to help ease her fear and give her peace before she died. I spoke with the social worker, and we agreed that it would be good for me to contact Sarah, who was helping with the care-giving in hopes of facilitating reconciliation. The daughter was surprised that her mother had expressed this concern, and she said she would do anything to help bring her mother peace of mind, but she knew that her sister would not. We agreed to meet the following morning at eight.

I entered the room with Sarah. I went to the bedside, greeted Lois, and told her why we had come together. I asked her if she wanted to make things right with her daughter, and she said she did. I then listened as mother and daughter shared a conversation of forgiveness that covered years of each mistreating the other. Both were able to verbalize love for the other, as well as the desire to forgive all that had gone before.

It was a moving experience to stand at that bedside and experience the grace of God working in and through the shared love of a mother and one of her daughters. This was a bittersweet moment because one daughter still refused her mother's love. It was a privilege to then lift them up in prayer. At the conclusion of my prayer, Lois said, "I'm ready to go now."

And the daughter replied, "And now, Mother, I'm ready to let you go."

Lessons for Caregivers

People may share the same spiritual heritage and may as a family physically relate to one other on a daily basis, yet they may still be living miles apart. Time passes and relational conflicts are ignored because the present circumstances permit each person to focus on something more demanding and more tolerable. For instance, both Lois and her daughter were greatly influenced by the Christian faith. Each knew and valued the teachings of the church that had molded their spiritual journeys. As family they also shared a past of mutual conflict, and both carried the scars of previous battles. Both had their regrets, which were best described in their confessions of "woulda, coulda, shoulda." But Lois's failing health thrust her daughter into the role of primary caregiver, and she fulfilled it out of her sense of duty and the knowledge that her sister was never coming home. Taking care of her mother's physical needs became the central focus of their communication and permitted them to ignore the deeper relational pain they had both experienced.

As Lois's health continued to deteriorate, she suffered from the knowledge that she might die without reconciling their relationship. She feared making things worse and causing a bigger rift between them, yet she didn't want to die without at least trying one more time.

The caregivers who were with Lois daily were alert enough to notice that her mood changed as she declined physically, and they were concerned. The restless fear they observed needed to be addressed by someone, and as a team they evaluated who would have the best opportunity to help her. That process provides an important lesson: Each dying person has many caregivers, and they must work as a team for the good of the patient. Each has developed a different level of trust with the patient, and knowing who does what best ensures that the patient will receive what is needed.

When you are the caregiver whom the patient trusts the most, you have both a tremendous responsibility as well as a wonderful opportunity. Because of the level of trust you have with the patient, you are able to be direct and confronting. When you sense that the person's life has been strongly shaped by religious values, you can ask questions and discern if the dying person has some unfinished business related to those values. When you are able to name the emotion you see in the patient, such as Lois's fear, then the patient can address that emotion. Once the patient finds the source of the emotional problem, she finds hope that maybe something can be done about the problem before she dies.

Once the caregiver and the patient agree about what the patient hopes will happen, then the caregiver must act to facilitate the process. In my experience, facilitating forgiveness becomes the means of freeing both the dying patient and those with whom she has struggled in relationship from future regret.

chapter 16

When Feelings Undermine Faith

Tears are okay. They are not a sign of weakness. Death, disappointment, loss, and blocked possibilities cause us to feel anguish. These feelings of pain in our grief are signs of our love.... If we had no love, we would not grieve. And to deny our grief is to deny our love.

—James L. Mayfield

JUST AS I REACHED OUT to ring the doorbell, the door opened and the husband of the patient I had come to visit welcomed me. I had spoken to him a few minutes earlier on the telephone. Richard's wife, Jane, was fifty-two years old and had been battling cancer for over two years. Over the past three weeks she had begun to decline physically and emotionally. Because of this change, it was recommended that she enter our hospice program. Richard had called our office requesting a pastoral counselor for his wife because she was anxious and depressed.

He thanked me for coming and led me into the small bedroom to meet his wife. When I entered, she apologized for not looking better. I tried to set her mind at ease by saying that I wasn't expecting her to get all "dolled up" for me. She forced a smile. I extended my hand and told her my name. She slid herself toward the middle of the bed and patted the bed, inviting me to sit down. As I sat down, her husband excused himself, giving us permission to talk alone.

There was the usual introductory moment of silence between us, and then I said, "Talk to me. Tell me what you've been thinking."

She immediately responded, "I know I'll be all right when I get there, but getting there is so hard."

In order to be sure I understood her, I asked, "Are you speaking about the difference between death and the process of dying?"

"Yes." She paused for a moment, then continued, "I have believed in God and understand that when I get there I'll be OK, but I guess I'm beginning to wonder."

"About what?" I asked.

"Well, I just don't have the feeling of peace I used to have."

"When did you last have that feeling of peace?"

"During these past two years I've been fine with this, but now I'm not feeling fine. I don't feel that peace, and I don't know what that means. I don't really know if I'm going to get there."

With that confession, her eyes began to redden and small tears silently began to form. I reached out and held her hand and said, "Let me reassure you, Jane, that God's love for you doesn't depend upon your feelings."

She said, "Are you sure?"

And I answered, "Yes, I'm very sure. The Scriptures teach us this in many places, and one of those verses says, 'While we were yet sinners, Christ died for us' (Rom. 5:8, KJV). That tells me that God's love was extended to us when we didn't feel very loving toward God, just as parents still love their children when the children misbehave."

She thought about that for a moment, attempted a smile, and said, "I want to believe that." Then she asked me where she would be after she died. She wanted to know if she would be in a state of sleep or if she would be alert.

I reminded her of the Scripture verse, "To be away from the body and at home with the Lord" (see 2 Cor. 5:8). I reminded her of the familiar closing verse of Psalm 23, "I will dwell in the house of the LORD forever" (23:6). I added to that Jesus' words about "going to prepare a place for us" (see John 14:2). I affirmed the truth of these verses: that God has a plan for us beyond this earthly existence, and although we can't describe it in detail, we accept it in faith. Then I asked, "Do you believe that?"

"Yes," she said. "I believe that, but my feelings..." She didn't finish, but I knew what she was saying. What she believed didn't filter down and take away her anxiousness. She then said, "I wish I could just go to sleep and not wake up. That would be peaceful."

We talked about any unfinished business she might have. It was difficult for her to talk about her two adult children and how she didn't want them to see her cry. We talked about the purpose of tears and how Jesus himself had cried when he grieved the death of his friend Lazarus, about how she needed to be honest with her family and not try to be strong for them, and about how tears were not so much a sign of weakness, but of love.

Before I left, I encouraged her to think about the years she had lived and the joys she had shared. She said, "My illness has made me realize how blessed I've been." I encouraged her to name those blessings and let her family know how blessed she felt. I prayed with her, and she thanked me for coming.

Before leaving the home, I sat in the living room and listened to Richard share with me his feelings of love and devotion for his wife. He was hopeful that our conversation would help her. I reminded him that we were available for both of them, that our team would be there for them as they continued their difficult grief work through the valley of the shadow.

Lessons for Caregivers

Disease that slowly destroys the cells of the body may also have a way of unraveling the fabric of faith. At such a time in one's spiritual journey, there is a struggle to believe that truth is not always defined by the gut. Jane was experiencing a new tension between what she knew intellectually to be true and the fact that she was unable to experientially validate those truths in her feelings. She, like so many who approach death, condensed her faith to the personal feeling of peace. She invested a great deal of her waking moments wondering if the lack of that feeling was an indication that she might not "make it."

And, although Jane had two adult children and a husband, I got the sense that she felt she had to be the "strong one" for the family. That is a tiring, lonely role that adds confusion to the feelings of the dying. Her husband's hope that my conversation with her would help raised a common concern. Often, a loving spouse feels inadequate in providing all that the patient needs. This helplessness, when expressed, becomes a shared hope that someone outside the family just might be able to offer the care that prepares the one who is dying for a peaceful death. Jane needed a caregiver who would give her reason to conclude that she was wrong about her feelings of doubt.

A caregiver who hears a patient speak about feeling sad, depressed, or uncertain about her faith needs to interpret such a conversation as a cry for help. Being able to listen and encourage the person to express those feelings and trace them back to where they began and when they changed will help the patient unload a part of the burden she carries. However, as helpful as that is, the caregiver must also be able to change the focus for the patient so that she can examine those feelings from a different perspective.

Also, it is important to reconnect the patient with her prior confidence in her faith values. The caregiver's knowledge of Scripture and the ability to use it as it relates to the patient's problem is a way to help the patient begin the journey back to where she once was. Familiar Scriptures became a convincing reminder to Jane that God's acceptance was not based on how we feel at any given moment any more than a parent's love for her child is based upon the feelings of the child when he is having a temper tantrum. God's love and promises remain solid, despite our feelings.

chapter 17

Caring for the Dying Agnostic

斷斷斷斷斷斷斷斷斷斷斷斷斷斷斷斷斷斷斷斷斷斷斷斷斷斷斷斷斷斷斷斷斷斷斷

*If learning means experience laced with questions that
still haunt ... if it means faith beyond knowledge of
what is seen ... if learning means recognizing reality but
not necessarily understanding it, yes, I've experienced
much learning.*

—R. F. Smith Jr.

MY HOSPICE PROGRAM holds that it is important to honor any
patient's religious preferences. At the time of their admission into
the program, they are asked to what degree they would desire our
pastoral counselors to visit them. Most check the box that indicates that our services are welcomed. At the time of our first visit,
we make an official assessment of the needs that our staff would
be most helpful in meeting. This assessment is added to the plan
of care in the patient's chart, and this provides our pastoral counseling staff with information that helps to assure continuity of care
for each patient and their families.

I was reading such a chart one morning when I discovered that
a patient had been admitted who checked the box "Not at this
time" when asked how helpful our pastoral counseling services
would be for her. I also noticed that written on the line where the
patient was to indicate her religion was one word: *agnostic.*
Noticing that the patient had been in the unit for several days and
that no assessment had been made, I thought it appropriate for me
to do the assessment and meet this patient.

I noted in her chart that her name was Joan. She was seventy-
three years old and suffering from heart disease. Upon my arrival in

her room, I discovered her sitting propped up in bed with several pillows. She had a pleasant smile for me as I told her who I was and the purpose of my visit. She invited me to sit down, and I pulled the chair closer to her bedside and began the assessment. In the process of filling in the blanks of the assessment form, I asked Joan to list a religious preference, and she responded, "Agnostic."

I asked her if she would mind telling me how she had reached that choice and how her belief helped her with knowing that she had a terminal illness. She gave me a brief and intelligent response, though her tone conveyed some uncertainty and I suspected some fears. I checked out my suspicion by asking, "Do I detect that you may be experiencing a bit of fear?"

She mustered a gentle smile and replied, "Aren't most people fearful given my situation?"

"Not always," I said. "Some are actually very much at peace because of their religious beliefs."

Her response was one of silence as she stared at the distant wall. I broke the silence by asking, "Joan, could I ask you a personal question?"

She turned and looked at me and said, "Yes."

"Are you an ordinary agnostic or an ornery agnostic?"

A smile broke across her face, and she said, "I don't know what you mean. What's the difference?"

I explained to her that I had met many people through the years who had declared themselves to be agnostic, and I had come to classify them in those two categories. The ordinary agnostic says, "I don't know if there is a God, but you might know." The ornery agnostic says, "I don't know if there is a God, and YOU DON"T EITHER!"

She turned away from me again and stared at the distant wall as she thought about the difference between the two types. I waited, and finally she responded, "I'm the ordinary kind."

I smiled and said, "I'm glad to hear that. Because you are ordinary you are willing to admit that although you don't know, someone else might. When I said earlier that some people are at peace with their dying, I was speaking about people who would tell you that they have a faith that gives them confidence in a loving God who has been with them in life and will be with them in death."

I stopped, allowing my words to register some acceptance or rejection on her face. She looked at me and said, "I guess that's the part that I just don't know."

I suggested that she think about this and said that I would stop by the next day so we could talk more. She welcomed the idea.

The next day Joan had questions about the Bible and the faith we had spoken of the day before. At the end of our conversation I commended her for her honest responses and her seeking heart and mind. I reminded her that my faith includes a God who loves each of us and desires that we accept that love. It includes a God with whom we have a relationship through prayer. It is in our praying that we can open ourselves up to God and invite him to forgive us our sins and experience his peace. I then asked her, "Would you allow me to pray for you?"

She smiled and said, "I would like that."

Following my prayer, she thanked me and I left.

When I arrived at the hospice the following weekend, I learned that Joan had died during the week. It's at such a time that my pastoral spirit is frustrated, because I am not privileged to share more of the journey through the valley of the shadow with an individual.

Lessons for Caregivers

The values and beliefs by which a person lives ought to provide her some comfort and assurance when she is facing death. Even people who are not connected to organized religion but who have lived by certain values and beliefs are very often at peace with themselves as they face death. Caregivers who come out of an organized, faith-based community need to be sensitive to how they can best support such a person. The caregivers may simply provide the emotional support of a presence at the bedside, or they may provide an opportunity for the patient to articulate how her values and beliefs are helpful to her now. To engage a person in discussion about her beliefs gives her the opportunity to hear herself and to either affirm those values or to question them. This caring dialogue provides her the opportunity to share end-of-life issues with someone who cares.

In this process, the caregiver looks for clues that indicate that the patient welcomes his support and then sorts out what support is needed. A small and seemingly insignificant clue was given when I first met Joan. After telling her who I was and why I was there, she invited me to sit down. Caregivers need to look for such clues because they signal the measure of acceptance that is being extended to them—and to some degree the unexpressed hope that the patient may want to discuss.

When the patient raises concerns or expresses fear or uncertainty about her beliefs, the caregiver may then appropriately share experiences and information that provide the patient with something to think about. If the patient's reservations about her values are acknowledged, it opens the door for the caregiver to share those religious teachings that have brought assurance and peace to others. When the caregiver proceeds in this way he shows respect for the patient and her beliefs, but also demonstrates for the patient how assurance and peace are possible.

chapter 18

The Vertical and Horizontal Relationships Are Important

When I am old, I hope I do not die between sterile sheets, hooked up to a respirator in a germ-free environment. I hope I'm on a tennis court, straining my heart with one last septuagenarian overhead smash.

—*Philip Yancey*

I MET LELA ON A SATURDAY morning. She was eighty-four years old, weighed about seventy-five pounds, had osteoporosis, and was bent over from the shoulders. She was sitting in her bed as I visited with the patient who shared her room. When I finished my visit, I stepped over to Lela's bed and introduced myself as the weekend pastoral counselor. "What is your name?" I asked.

She lifted her head as best she could, and, making eye contact, responded, "Are you testing me?"

I took that to mean that she wondered if I was attempting to discover how sharp she was mentally, so I replied, "No, I'm not testing you. I don't know your name. I haven't seen your chart, but since you were awake I thought I'd stop and meet you."

Then she asked, "First or last?"

I said, "Let's start with the first name, and then give me the last."

From that introduction, I could tell that although Lela's body was frail and suffering from disease, her mind was very sharp. We talked for fifteen minutes or so about her family and her faith. She told me that two of her children were out on the patio if I'd like to meet them, and when I left I went and introduced myself to them. They spoke quite highly of their mother and of many of her life accomplishments.

The following weekend when I went into Lela's room to see her, she was not there. I inquired about her to the nurse, who said that Lela was no doubt out on the patio since she loved the outdoors. I stepped out onto the patio where I found Lela seated in a chair, bent over with her face nearly touching her knees. I spoke her name, and her head slowly lifted. I reminded her who I was, and she said, "I know, I know, we visited last week."

As we talked of many things, our conversation eventually turned to God, and I asked, "Lela, are you at peace with God?"

She again looked me directly in the eyes and said, "I didn't know we had quarreled."

I smiled and told her I liked that answer. I asked her if there was any Scripture she would like to have read to her, and she thought for a moment, then said, "Read the twenty-third."

So I read her the twenty-third Psalm and, as I was reading it, a white dove landed behind her chair and within two feet of me. It walked around under her chair and next to mine. When I finished reading the Psalm, I asked, "Do you see what I see?"

She nodded her head and said, "It's a superstition."

"What's a superstition?" I responded.

"The white dove."

I thought for a moment and remembered that a white dove had appeared several months ago at the same care unit and stayed by the window of a dying patient's room. I said to Lela, "Is it a good or bad superstition?"

She said, "It's bad."

"Can you tell me why?" I inquired.

"Someone's going to die," she said.

We shared a few moments of silence, and then I took her hand and asked her, "If it is you, Lela, are you ready?"

She said, "Not quite yet."

"Do you still have something to do or people to see?" I asked.

She said, "Yes, I have things I want to say to people before I go."

I reminded her that she had the gift of time and a good mind with which to do what she needed to do, and I encouraged her not to let opportunities pass. I prayed with her that she would have the chance to share what was on her heart and mind with her family as they visited with her. I left confident that she would heed this advice and that she still had time—and the mental and physical capacity—to do so.

Lessons for Caregivers

Lela's story is proof that a person can continue to exhibit the same personality traits when facing death as she did throughout her life. Her straightforward, humorous manner of communication was not put on the shelf because she was dying. Instead, it continued even as she responded to the more serious questions regarding her relationship with God. Most people respond to the question about being at peace with God with a simple yes, but Lela revealed her confidence with a response that stated more. She was making it clear that she and God were old friends and there was nothing between them that needed to be made right. A caregiver's affirmation of that kind of confidence is important.

There is an additional lesson to be gleaned from this story. Caregivers ought to be aware of two dimensions of a patient's life: the vertical and the horizontal. Each dimension defines an important kind of relationship in the patient's spiritual journey. Lela's vertical connection with God was where she knew it should be, but, as we have seen with others, she wasn't ready to die just yet because her horizontal relationships with others needed some attention.

The caregiver who hears that there is unfinished business relating to the patient's horizontal relationships with others should assess how much time the patient might have to work on those issues and should also assess the physical and mental ability of the patient to achieve this goal. In Lela's case, it appeared that time, as well as her physical and mental abilities, were in her favor. She, unlike many who enter our hospice, was able to deal with her unfinished business early in her illness, while her mental faculties were still sharp. Caring for Lela meant being able to help her identify the unfinished business in her life and remind her of the gift of time that she had in which to deal with that business.

When a patient makes any statement that can have a variety of meanings, it is good for the caregiver to allow the patient to clarify what she means by it, instead of drawing conclusions from the caregiver's own experience. It is often conversation about symbolic subjects, introduced by the dying person, that provides the best insights into where she is in the process. The white dove was to Lela a reminder that she shouldn't wait too long to take care of her unfinished business.

And the white dove was a reminder to me of my own mortality and the gift of time I also had. Caregivers always have the opportunity to learn from the dying how fragile life is and how important it is to apply the same lessons to themselves.

chapter 19

Helping a Grieving Family

*Benjamin Franklin was taking his customary walk…. A
young admirer greeted him with the question: "And how
is Mr. Franklin today?" The old gentleman responded,
"Well, the house in which he lives is in a growing state of
disrepair…. But, Mr. Franklin is very well."*

—Herbert N. Conley

I WAS CALLED TO the hospice unit to offer a prayer with a Navajo family whose ninety-seven-year-old mother had just died. When I arrived, some of the family members were in the lounge, while several of the woman's sons were in the room, where her body still lay on the bed. I identified myself and asked if they would like to gather in the room to share a time of reflecting about their mother. They responded positively to the suggestion. Twelve of us gathered in the room, some in chairs and some standing. I stood by the bedside and began by asking, "What would you like to tell me about your mother that would help me to know her and help you celebrate her life?"

One of the woman's daughters, who had been the primary caregiver over the past ten years, spoke up. "Mom was a very giving person. She gave to each of us and to others in the church and the community. She loved people. She's going to be missed."

Another daughter added, "Here is a poem that tells you exactly how we feel about our mother. I'd like you to read it for all of us."

I took the sheet of paper and read:

*Blessed is the mother who follows the Lord,
so her children can learn and can grow.*

The unselfish mother who holds on with love,
Yet knows when it's time to let go.
Blessed is the mother who's
patient, forgiving,
The one who cannot bear a grudge,
The one who accepts people just as they are
Without stopping to question or judge.
Blessed is the mother whose faith keeps her going
Through trials and traumas and cares,
Who handles the easy with wisdom and love
And the not-quite-so easy with prayers.
Blessed is the mother who meets all your needs
From the very first day of your birth,
Blessed is the mother, who shares so much love,
For she's God's special angel on earth.

When I finished, one of the woman's sons said, "She is the one who passed on to us the love that she knew from God. She is the one who told us about Jesus and his love for us, and she showed us how important it was for us to pass it on to our children also."

The others in the room nodded their heads in agreement, smiles on their faces. We stood and joined hands, and I offered a prayer of thanksgiving for the love that was shared in their family. Then I asked for the Spirit to surround the family as they journeyed together through the valley of the dark shadow.

After I left, I reflected on the fact that within the Native American culture, it is important to pass on to the next generation those things that were valued by the previous generation. It is important for them to instruct their children in the ways of their culture so that they will be able to appreciate the values that have shaped their community. This can be seen in the way that a Native American mother teaches her daughter how to weave a basket or in how a daughter or a son is taught the art of making jewelry or pottery. Families of any culture often create customs and traditions that they pass on to the next generation, and the way they celebrate holidays often provides a glimpse into those traditions. Native Americans, however, exhibit this generational bonding with more than holiday customs and tribal crafts and skills. They also place a high priority on their religious practices. That deep desire to pass things on also includes the values of their faith.

The Navajo mother had lived through ninety-seven years of great change. She had to raise her children to value their tribal customs and traditions even as they were introduced to an American culture that challenged them. Her own spiritual journey of discovering the true God, rather than "The Great Spirit and Creator of the Earth," was a legacy she imparted to her children. The threads of her children's spiritual journeys were strongly woven into the fabric of hers, and their very lives were like vessels of pottery shaped by her gentle touch.

The children's tribute to their mother's spiritual influence on their lives reminded me of the day when my wife and I sat before a judge at the final adoption hearing of one of our children. The judge had asked us, "How willing are you to accept this child as one to whom you will leave your inheritance?" And then, before we could answer, he peered over his reading glasses and, with a smile on his face, said, "Seeing that you're a clergyman, I suspect that won't be much."

Feeling that his remark was totally inappropriate, I couldn't help responding, "Judge, that depends on how you define inheritance, doesn't it?"

He slowly nodded his head in agreement and said, "Yes, I suppose it does."

Parents, by nature of their job descriptions in any culture, are expected to shape the attitudes, values, and behavior of their children. How wonderful for that Navajo mother's family that she did her job well.

Lessons for Caregivers

Death has an impact on families in a variety of ways, and a caregiver who does not know the family must find a way to encourage them to reveal what that impact has been in order best to help the family through this time. One way to do this is to gather the family at the bedside of the deceased and ask each of them to share some memory or word that would help you as the caregiver to gain a brief glimpse into just who this person was to them. Through the telling of their stories, the relationships they each shared with the deceased will soon become evident.

It is important for caregivers outside the family network to recognize and affirm the wonderful gift that the family has been given in the deceased and to remind them of how their lives will continue to reflect the influences of the one who has died. This was not hard to do in the instance above, for in the Navajo community, when a matriarch or a patriarch dies there is a sense of loss of the leader who was responsible not only for giving birth to the family, but also for setting the standards by which that family lived. The Navajo mother had been the significant influence in shaping the values and beliefs of each of her children and grandchildren. Contributions of the deceased may not always be so readily evident, but caregivers do well to identify them.

Family members need the support of caregivers at the time of death even though the death has been anticipated. They have been working through their grief, but the death always begins a new phase as they move from anticipation to the reality and finality that death brings. It is a good time to encourage them to begin speaking of their loved one in the past tense, and they can do that most easily if a caregiver invites them to share a memory or tell a story. They may find such a moment even more memorable than the formal funeral or memorial service.

chapter 20

Moving from Doubt to Faith

━━━━━━━━━━━━━━━━━━━━━━━━━━━━━━━━━━━━━

> *At one time, men built*
> *palaces of stone,*
> *elaborate mausoleums,*
> *as their way of commemorating*
> *their dead.*
>
> *There are other ways to perpetuate*
> *the memory of your loved one.*
> *Through your own life*
> *you can prolong the memory.*
> —Earl A. Grollman

FAMILY COMMUNICATION is unique to individual families. Some families are composed of members who are quiet, private individuals. Even though they share a common space, they respect one another's solitude. Communication within this type of family is mostly centered on coordinating and meeting the practical, day-to-day needs. Children in this type of family often grow into adulthood and at some point realize that they don't know much about their parents. They value what was taught to them and what their parents mean to them, but they admit that they don't know much about their parents' personal beliefs and convictions.

Such was the case with Faith's family. Faith was eighty-seven years old and dying.

"If you could come and talk with Mother, I think we'd all feel better," her concerned son, Mark, began his conversation with me over the telephone. "I don't know if she has prayed the *sinners prayer.*"

As intimate as family members may be, there are times when they are not sure about one another's spiritual journeys. The son who made this request shared his own personal belief and convictions with me about salvation, and he said that he needed to know if his mother had ever prayed the "sinner's prayer." His brother and sister were in agreement with this desire. These were adult children in their fifties. I told the son I would be there in about thirty minutes.

When I arrived, I met the other brother and sister in the lounge. I clarified the request with them and suggested that they not be in the room when I talked with their mother. They all agreed. They said that their father was in the room, sitting at the bedside with their mother, who was alert and talking. They offered to go into the room with me to meet their parents.

As we gathered at the bedside, Mark introduced me to his father, Harry, and his mother. He then said that he and his siblings would leave and allow me to speak with their mother. Harry got up to leave with them, but I said, "Why don't you stay and share this time with us?" He sat back down and again took his wife's hand.

As the other family members left the room, I sat in a chair by the bed. After a brief silence, I said to Faith, "Where did you get the name Faith?"

She moistened her lips, obviously dried from medications, and replied, "My mother was a religious woman, and her father was a minister."

"It sounds to me like you had a very thoughtful, caring mother," I replied.

"I sure did," she said with a twinkle in her eyes, indicating that it was pleasant for her to remember her mother.

After a brief pause, I asked her, "Are those religious teachings that you grew up with helpful at this particular time, in your condition?"

Her immediate smile and response were very convincing. She said, "Yes, they certainly are. I know God loves me, and God knows I love him. I pray every day."

I responded by saying that she must then know about God's wonderful forgiveness offered to each of us. She said, "I not only know about it, I've experienced it."

I affirmed her statement of faith and her love for God and her family. Harry and I held her hands, and I offered a prayer on their behalf.

I said good-bye and returned to the lounge where the other family members had gone. I shared with them a summary of our conversation and the statement of faith their mother had made. They expressed an appreciation for my coming.

During the next two days, their patterns of communication changed, and they grew more comfortable with sharing with one another. During this time, they discovered a lot about their mother that they hadn't known.

Faith died the following Wednesday, and Mark asked the unit staff to contact me and see if I would conduct his mother's funeral. At the service, the family shared with me that just before Faith died, she had awakened and asked that all the family gather at her bedside. When they were all there, she spoke in a very clear and strong voice, telling them how much she loved them and how they were to love one another. Shortly after that, she died. It was a final memory of her that they could treasure.

Because of this memorable moment, the family asked that I conclude the funeral service with the reassuring Scripture from 1 John 4:7, 11: "Beloved, let us love one another, because love is from God; everyone who loves is born of God and knows God.... Beloved, since God loved us so much, we also ought to love one another."

Each of them felt that it was their mother's legacy.

Lessons for Caregivers

A terminal diagnosis gets the attention of every member of a family. How they deal with the information and communicate with one another most often is a continuation of the patterns that have already been created in their family relationships. This was evident when Faith's adult children did not feel comfortable sharing with their mother their desire to know more about her spiritual journey. For some reason, the topic was off limits. They did, however, feel strongly enough about it that they talked among themselves about what to do and shared their concern with the nurse on duty.

Caregivers of the dying need to be sensitive to family members and hear their concerns, hopes, and fears. There will be times when the end-of-life issues they are dealing with will relate to unresolved matters with the person who is dying. When a caregiver hears such a concern expressed, it is important to discuss ways that the matter can be resolved and to offer to assist in resolving it. To resolve such matters provides both the dying person and the family members a peace that will prevent them from living with regrets.

It is important for the caregiver to listen to how the family's concerns are verbalized; he can learn a lot from the vocabulary that is used as well as from the tone in which the concerns are shared. Mark expressed his concern about his mother to me with a religious vocabulary that told me there were some conservative Christian influences within the family. It was obvious to me that Faith's adult children knew the value of their own spiritual journeys but did not know if their mother shared a common experience. Given the terminal nature of her disease and the limited time remaining, they wanted to be assured of their mother's salvation.

The caregiver also needs to handle the family's need based on what he or she has learned from those who expressed the concern. Faith's children knew that it would be best if I spoke alone with their mother and father and addressed their concern, rather than their making a direct request of her. In such a situation, there is no reason for a caregiver to create any additional problems by identifying the source of the concern, since the matter can simply be addressed through a caring conversation.

chapter 21

The Fear of God's Rejection Too

━━━

If we...can help the patient and his family to get "in tune" to each other's needs...we can help to avoid much unnecessary agony and suffering on the part of the dying and even more so on the part of the family that is left behind.

—Elisabeth Kübler-Ross

ON MY PAGER WAS a message with the name of a patient with AIDS and a telephone number to call to confirm the patient's request for a pastoral counselor. The person who answered the telephone was not the patient, but a man who identified himself as Theodore. He confirmed that the patient, Michael, was expecting a pastoral counselor, and he gave me directions to their condominium. Theodore said that when I arrived there would be someone at the desk in the lobby who could direct me to their condo, or I could use my cell phone and call for someone to meet me in the lobby.

The twenty-minute drive gave me the opportunity to anticipate what the needs of the patient might be, as this was not a typical call. When I arrived, I was greeted in the lobby by a man named James, a friend of both Michael's and Theodore's. We went to the condo, and Michael's friends called for him. James apologized for the apartment being a mess, explaining that they had just moved in the day before and had a lot of unpacking to do.

Michael came into the living room and introduced himself. His glassy eyes indicated that he was either in pain or on heavy painkillers—or possibly both. He reached out his hand and thanked me for coming. He said, "I'd like to find a private place for us to talk." Theodore suggested that we go to the fitness room down the hall.

I helped Michael walk down the hall to the fitness room, where there were several tables at the end of the room. We sat across from each other.

"I feel so abandoned," Michael said, in a deep Southern drawl. And then he began to sob. He continued, "I've been abandoned all my life, ever since I was a teenager."

Michael continued to sob as he told me that, as a teenager, he'd lost a friend, in fact his lover, to AIDS. He went on to say that people had been abandoning him ever since. "My momma and daddy don't understand me. I call my momma, and she tells me all I ever have is bad news so don't call. My daddy's dead as far as I'm concerned, because he's a lying preacher who doesn't begin to know what it means to love. I even feel like God's abandoned me.... Why does God let this all happen to me?"

It was clear to me that to this point Michael had had a very difficult life, a very troubled life that resulted in decisions he now regretted. I focused on my role of ministering to him in his time of need as opposed to judging or questioning how he'd gotten to this point.

We sat in silence for a few moments, and then I said, "Michael, I don't presume to know the answer to your question. I wish I had an answer. Is there anything good happening to you at all?"

Michael responded by saying that at least he had a few friends, including James and Theodore. After a few moments of silence, I asked, "Michael, why did you want to see a pastoral counselor?"

"I don't know. I guess I want to be sure that God really does love me even though I get angry at him, because he doesn't seem to show it. I guess it's because I'm scared, and I don't want to die. I love God, and I know God knows I love him."

"How familiar are you with the Bible?" I asked.

"I know the Bible, and I've read it all my life. That's how I know God does love me, but I just need someone to tell me he really does love me," Michael said as he began to sob harder.

I shared some Scriptures with Michael about God's love and about God's promises to never give up on us. I asked him if he would claim those promises and accept God's love and forgiveness. He assured me that he had accepted God's love and forgiveness, and he asked me to pray with him.

After we had prayed, we went back to the condo, and I said my good-byes and took the elevator down to the lobby. As I drove to my next call, I reflected on Michael, his lifestyle, and his experience of faith. I was again made aware of how different the situations are to which I am called, yet how similar in that people desire to have the assurance that they are not alone as they face their deaths. They want to be reassured that God cares about them, and they want to hear that from another person whom they trust.

Several weeks passed, and then one Saturday morning I saw Michael's name on the patient board of one of our units. When I entered his room, I could see that he was still battling the pain of his disease, but he was alert and turned his head to greet me. I reminded him who I was, and he said, "I remember."

After a brief conversation to get reacquainted, I asked him, "Has anything good been happening to you since I saw you last?"

He started to cry and said, "Yes, I talked with my daddy last night, and he told me he loves me."

As he continued to cry, I said, "That must be about the best news you've heard lately."

"That's the only good news I've heard lately," he responded. He went on to say, without explanation, that Theodore and James had "given up" on him, leaving him pretty much alone.

"I hope you haven't forgotten the Scriptures we shared together last time that remind us that God never gives up on us."

"No," he said, "I haven't forgotten, but I still have times when I doubt it. Will you pray for me?"

Following the prayer, I said good-bye. Michael's spiritual journey was a struggle with past decisions and relationships that he longed to resolve before he died, even though he knew they would not all be resolved. His journey held a mixture of hope that his suffering would stop and a fear that when it did, he might discover that God had also given up on him. Can the valley of the shadow get much darker than that?

Lessons for Caregivers

Some people may never fully find the peace that they are looking for before they die. Some may never have the hurtful relationships in their lives resolved. Some may never fully accept the truth that they know in their minds regarding the beliefs they have been taught. Some desire to be free from the painful process of dying, but the fear of what is in store for them after death creates a great deal of anxiety.

The caregiver who sits with such a person will feel the helplessness of having little to offer that will change the circumstances for the dying patient. The great temptation for the caregiver will be to stay away from such a situation because there is little satisfaction in not having any answers. But to stay away is to reinforce the patient's feeling of being abandoned. When a person experiences loneliness and estrangement from parents and friends, it is easy for him to reach the conclusion that God will also abandon him. A foundational knowledge of the Scriptures seems to be a two-edged sword for a person like this. He finds promises in the Scriptures that he wants to claim, but these promises may be mixed with a sense that he feels he may face rejection.

Caregivers providing reminders of those Scriptures can help to reinforce the truth of God's love and care, although the caregiver must remember that such torment of the spirit cannot be relieved by a simple quote from Scripture. Michael is not unlike many others who approach death and have no one who cares. As caregivers, we learn from them that their greatest need is not to have someone provide answers to questions, but to have someone to be present and share their struggle to the extent possible.

chapter 22

From Agitation to Confession

In helping others to solve the inexplicability of non-existence, we strengthen ourselves in the realization that dying and death are phases of life and living. Each one of us is a helper—the parent, the physician, the counselor, the clergyman, the attorney, the funeral director, the insurance agent, the teacher, the neighbor, the friend—you!

—*Earl A. Grollman*

THE FRAIL, NINETY-THREE-YEAR-OLD man was restless, displaying his agitation with movements and mutterings that concerned his daughter-in-law as she stood at his bedside stroking his back, seeking to calm him. I stood at the door of his room watching until she realized someone was there. When she noticed me, I said, "I'm the pastoral counselor from Hospice of the Valley. Is this patient Francis Rhodes?"

"Yes, this is Francis," she replied. "I'm the one who asked the nurse to send us a pastor. I'm his daughter-in-law, Lena, and this is his son, John."

John stood and extended his hand to greet me. I knew nothing about Francis except that he had been admitted to our hospice the day before. As we talked I learned that he had been in this particular skilled nursing facility for two years. Over the past several weeks he had begun to show noticeable decline in his physical condition. Because of his restlessness, his family was advised that he could possibly decline very rapidly, and Lena thought that it would be good to have a pastor come and pray with him.

In our conversation I learned that Francis, some years ago, had been "saved." I offered to pray with Francis.

Lena responded, "He's hard of hearing, so you'll have to speak near his ear."

I went close to the head of the bed and reached out with my arm so that I could stroke Francis's back as he continued to move restlessly. I told him, "Francis, I'm the pastor, and I've come to pray with you."

"Oh, Lord, oh, Lord," Francis said.

I began my prayer by offering thanks to God for Francis, for the gift of ninety-three years of life in which he had known the love of his family and friends, for the knowledge of God's love and for Francis's acceptance of the forgiveness that God had offered him. As I prayed, I noticed that Francis became less restless. I continued to pray, and he grew calmer. When Francis appeared to finally be relaxed I said, "Amen."

He responded immediately with, "Lord, have mercy on my soul; Lord, have mercy on my soul." He repeated this several times as I continued to hold his hand and pat his back. When he quieted down, I stepped away from the bed.

Lena said, "I can't believe he is this calm. He hasn't been this still for days. He appears to be very peaceful. Do you suppose he wanted someone to pray with him?"

"I don't know what he may have wanted," I replied, "but his words, 'Lord, have mercy on my soul,' are something that he has surely been thinking about. He was obviously connecting with the importance of prayer and seems to be showing that this has been a personally satisfying experience. His outward peaceful calm just may reflect that inner peace he has now experienced."

"Thank you so much," Lena said.

"I appreciate you calling and asking for a pastor," I responded. "You have given Francis a very special gift by caring for him in this way. If there's any more we can do to help, please call us again."

Lessons for Caregivers

Nursing homes are not pleasant places, but they are necessary places. Seeing people slouching in wheelchairs, hearing them cry out in desperate tones, and watching their hollow stares can quickly cause us to devalue their importance. Because little can be done to alter their physical discomfort, it is tempting to conclude that in the warehouse of the frail and aging, nothing can be done to alter patients' spiritual well-being either. Caregivers must be careful not to come to this inaccurate conclusion.

Caring in such a facility under such discouraging circumstances demands some creativity on the part of those who want the best for their loved ones. A simple way to exercise this creativity may be to identify something the patient valued during his former years and offer it in the hope that it will connect with him in some special way and provide a measure of peace. Because Francis had a history of being religious, his care-giving daughter-in-law hoped that the simple religious ritual of prayer would be of some comfort to him, so she made the call and asked for a visit from a pastoral counselor.

I recall another experience during my pastoral ministry when I was serving communion to a group of people in a nursing home during a Sunday afternoon "church service." As I took the bread and dipped it in the cup of wine and placed it on their lips, I spoke the familiar words of Jesus, "This is my body, and this is my blood shed for you." When I spoke those words to one woman who was always wheeled into the room but never showed any sign of alertness, tears began to form in her eyes. I did not know her background and to this day do not know what she was thinking, but I have concluded that something in the familiar religious ritual connected with her spiritual journey and triggered a feeling of joy for her.

When caregivers are invited to share a particular religious ritual with a patient, it is important to speak directly to the patient, introducing yourself and your religious title. It is often the familiar religious title that registers and gives the patient an awareness of having a "pastor" present to care for him. Informing the patient of what is going to be done shows respect for the patient and testifies to treatment full of dignity and grace.

During prayer, it is helpful to make physical contact with the patient. By holding the patient's hand and supporting him with an arm around the shoulders, the caregiver is able to monitor how the patient is responding to the prayer. In addition, by adding touch to the experience, the caregiver may be able to provide the patient with a sense of peace that will enable him to reach a state of calm. The mysterious communication of prayer provided Francis with a measure of comfort that transformed his restlessness into a litany of confession and hope.

Francis was comforted by a prayer and responded with the confession, "Lord, have mercy on my soul." St. Francis of Assisi could not have said it any better.

chapter 23

When the One Dying Is a Personal Friend

Work on the realms of spirit and soul is, of course, influenced by one's culture, religious tradition, family life, philosophical perspective, and life experiences, but it is inherently intimate and deeply personal.

—Ira Byock

ROBIN WAS MORE to me than a hospice patient whom I would visit only once. He was a personal friend. Upon hearing the diagnosis of cancer, he, like so many others, was determined to do all he could to arrest the condition. He took the recommended treatments and for over a year continued to get out of bed every morning and go off to the office and manage the business that he and his wife, Anne, shared.

Then came the dreaded day when Robin and Anne were told that not much more could be done medically. They explored with me the process of enrolling in our hospice program and requested that I be their pastoral counselor. They signed on for our services, and in the months that followed, Robin, Anne, and I shared many intimate moments together. Some of those moments we spent sitting in their living room sipping tea together and listening to the ways in which they were taking this journey together. Other moments involved worshiping in the same church pew and sharing in communion bread and wine together. This shared intimacy created a unique relationship unlike any other I have shared with a patient.

When Robin was transferred to one of our palliative care units for the first time, it signaled a change in his physical condition and led him to reflect on end-of-life issues. As he shared with me his thoughts and concerns, his choice of words signaled his movement toward accepting the reality of his disease. When I first entered his room and sat on his bed, he spoke softly the words, "I guess this is the last chapter."

"Yes," I said, "and you have a lot to say about what will be written."

After a reflective pause he said, "I suppose I do, but I'm going to need some help. You'll help me, won't you?"

"Yes, Robin, you can count on me being here to help you." After another brief moment of silence between us I said, "You've already been writing that chapter, haven't you?"

"I suppose so, but I want to have some time to write a bit more," he said hopefully.

"What are some of those areas that you need to write about?" I asked, hoping to help him focus on the specifics that he wanted to accomplish before he died.

"Well, I literally need to take care of my business and help Anne sort out just how to take care of everything. She doesn't use the computer very much, and there's stuff she'll need to access regarding the business and finances."

"Have you discussed any of this with her?" I inquired.

"No, not very much. She's been reluctant to tackle it. I've tried to encourage her, but I guess we both always felt there would be more time."

"How about we set a plan for getting that done?" I suggested.

"I guess we'd better. I'm thinking my son Scott would be a big help since he knows quite a bit about computers."

He then talked at length about what needed to be done, listing the things, for example, that needed to be accessed with passwords, etc. He soon showed an excitement in formulating a plan and was eager to share it with his son and wife when they visited that day.

When I returned a few days later, I discovered that Robin had set the plan in motion and they were working on the areas that concerned him. I commended him for his effort and said, "It looks like you're putting some substance into that last chapter you said you are writing."

"It's a beginning," he said, indicating that there were other issues that needed to be addressed.

In hopes of encouraging him to continue his effort, I asked, "What else have you been thinking about that you would like to be sure is included in this last chapter?"

"I'm not sure how to put this, Bill," he said, "but maybe you can help me sort it out. I need a plan on how to leave a legacy."

I wanted him to say more about what he was thinking, so I inquired, "Tell me, Robin, what you mean by a legacy."

"That's were I need your help," he replied, and then continued, "I'm not sure what it is I can do that kind of makes sense out of my life, that I will leave for others. Is this making any sense?"

"Yes," I responded. "I'm hearing you say that you want to be assured that the life you have lived will in some special way have made a difference."

"That's right on," he said with a smile.

"Robin, let me ask you a question that may sound like it's not at all on the same page as your concern. When is the best time to plant a tree?"

The glint in his eye told me that he was curious to see where I was going with this. He said, "I'd say this coming spring."

"No," I replied, "not this coming spring. The best time to plant a tree was twenty-five years ago. Do you know why?"

After a brief time of thoughtful reflection he said, "Well, it would be pretty well grown by now."

"That's exactly right, and I think leaving a legacy is like planting a tree. Your life legacy had its seeds planted many years ago, and in the future your friends and family will enjoy the fruit of that legacy. When your friends and family talk to me about you, they speak in loving words that affirm not only the high standards of integrity they've witnessed, but also the compassion you have shown for them. They have also known that those convictions come from a personal faith in God and the fellowship of the community of faith, the church."

After giving Robin a few moments to soak that all in, I continued, "So, you see, you've already got a legacy, and that is validated in many ways by the relationships you have shared. Think of the people who have stepped forward to assist you and Anne since you began this journey a couple of years ago. Each of them in his own way wants to do whatever he can because he cares about you and the friendship he has shared with you through the years. You see, your last chapter isn't something you write by yourself. Others are also providing content that helps define and validate the life you have lived."

Because humility also was part of his legacy, Robin showed uneasiness in agreeing with me, but his smile indicated that he appreciated what I said. His eyes also showed the effects of the morphine he had taken during my visit, so I suggested that we pray together and then I'd leave so he could rest. After we prayed, Robin thanked me and said, "This chapter is to be continued."

That chapter *was* continued for several weeks. Robin was able to go home; he even spent one morning back at his office. He included in his last chapter helping Anne find a smaller house in the same general area where she'd be close to her friends.

Lessons for Caregivers

There are two lessons to be gleaned from this story. First, when there is a close friendship between the caregiver and the dying person, it is not always easy to discuss end-of-life issues. To do so requires a shared understanding of the friend's willingness to accept the role of caregiver. The subject may be approached by either one, and in that conversation they should agree that each will be open and honest as they share the journey together.

From that day on, the relationship of friend as caregiver will take on new meaning. There will still be times when the patient and the caregiver friend share routine experiences together and there is no discussion about end-of-life issues, and those times will become sacred because they know that their time together is limited.

The caregiver friend will pay close attention to physical changes and be available to assist in whatever way possible. Because of the honesty agreement they share, the day will come when one of them will initiate a conversation about the end being near. That may come as it did in my case with the safe language Robin used about writing the last chapter in his book. Such language gives both people a chance to be honest and helpful as they discuss the impending death without having to use the more harsh vocabulary of death. What matters most is that both patient and caregiver friend are on the same page in the book.

Second, there is something to be learned from Robin's desire to leave some kind of legacy. Everyone appreciates knowing that his or her life has meaning. Those who are dying go through a life review and often need to be reminded of the contributions they have made to their families and communities. Robin felt confident enough in our relationship to be direct in asking me how he could be sure he would leave a legacy. Others may not be so direct, but caregivers can be sure that such affirmation will help patients know that their lives have had meaning. The time it takes to do a life review will depend on the anticipated time available and the willingness of the caregiver to commit to sharing in it. Not doing it all in one visit can provide the dying person with time to process what has been shared and allows him to look forward to the promised next meeting.

chapter 24

Comfort Is Not Always Explainable

<hr/>

*We are impatient with persons who want to give us the-
ology lessons in the midst of our grief. This may be so
because we are intuitively aware that what we need is
faith, and faith does not come at the end of an argument. How faith comes to us is a mystery.*

— *James L. Mayfield*

AN EIGHTY-THREE-YEAR-OLD Italian woman died in one of our
palliative care units, and her daughter, Rose, and granddaughter,
Rita, were struggling with their overwhelming grief. The nurse on
duty requested that I come to support them. When I entered the
room, the women were sobbing. I introduced myself and then
asked Rose if she would share with me how long her mother had
been ill and if her death had been peaceful.

After taking one more tissue and wiping her eyes, she began. "Just
last week we traveled together to Utah to visit my other daughter,
Laurie, and had such a wonderful time. We learned that she is
expecting a baby, and it's going to be a girl, and that made Mother
so happy that she was going to have a great-granddaughter."

She wiped her eyes again and continued, "When we arrived
back home, Mother wasn't feeling very well, and after visiting a
doctor we discovered that she had massive cancer throughout her
body. He gave us no hope for treatment to improve her condition
… and that was just last week."

When she recalled the moment when they had received that
shocking news, she again became overwhelmed with grief. "I'm so
sorry," she said, apologizing for not being in control of her emotions.

"But it has all happened so quickly, and I'm just not ready for this."

She took several deep breaths and forced a smile. I asked her if she would mind telling me about her mother. "What will be the special memories? What will you miss?" I asked.

The granddaughter, Rita, immediately said, "I'll never eat a good meal again. Sorry, Mom, but we both know that Grandma was the best cook in the world."

This made Rose smile; she knew the truth of what her daughter had just said. The granddaughter continued, "Her meatball spaghetti was the best."

Rose added, "Yes, and as often as I've tried to make it like she did, I could never get it just right. We will all miss Mom's cooking."

"Tell me what her interests were and if she had any particular work outside the home that she found satisfying," I inquired.

"Well, she wanted to be a biochemist, but due to health problems she had to give up that dream. She is a college graduate, as are her four brothers and two sisters. Some are doctors, another is a lawyer. Because she has a son who has disabilities she became interested in promoting an advocacy alliance for him and others, and what she began is now being done in many states."

I could see that sharing these memories with me was beginning to help the daughter and granddaughter focus on how much the deceased had meant not only to them but to many others who would miss her.

"The main work that she did was secretarial office work for the Catholic Church. And all of this happened so fast that we didn't even contact the priest," Rose said with some regret. Then she added, "But we know she's in a better place, where Daddy is."

"How long has it been since your father died?" I asked.

"Ten years," she answered. "But something really strange happened just before Mom died that made both my daughter and me feel a little bit better, although it was very strange and we don't understand it."

"Would you mind sharing that with me?" I asked.

"Well," she began, "we were both sitting with Mother, one of us on each side of the bed, just where we are now, and we both noticed the odor of a sweet-smelling pipe. We immediately looked at each other, having the same thought. We both thought about Grandpa, who always smoked a pipe, and the smell was just like he was here in this room. It only lasted a short time, and then Mother's breathing stopped and I called the nurse, and she said that Mother had just passed."

After trying to take in that mysterious, unexplainable experience, I inquired, "And what do you think that all means?"

"I think Daddy came for her. I know that sounds strange, and I can't begin to understand it, but we both experienced it and ..." Her explanation remained unfinished. "I know that, whatever it was, it has made me feel like all is well with her and she is at peace where Daddy is."

Following a period of silence I asked, "Would you like to share a prayer together, thanking God for her life and committing her to God's eternal keeping?"

"Yes," she said. "We'd like that."

We stood at the bedside holding hands as I gathered the experiences this daughter and granddaughter had expressed and offered a prayer on their behalf. I gave them each a hug, conveying my sympathy, and at their request I went out to the desk to inform the nurse that they were ready for the mortuary to be called.

For the next couple of days I couldn't get them out of my mind as I wondered about the strange experience they'd had of smelling the sweet fragrance of a pipe just before their mother (and grandmother) died. I had never heard or read of anything like that, and without some kind of confirmation from other sources I struggled to know what it was they had experienced.

A couple of days later while reading the book *Stress, Loss, & Grief* by John Schneider, I discovered in his chapter "Transforming

Grief" an experience that he calls "Transpersonal Consciousness." He writes, "People often discover ways in which they are open to the energies of others that extend beyond the usual forms of communication and contact." He gives the examples of visions or hearing the deceased person's voice and explains that such an experience usually enables the person who is grieving to process the loss and move toward acceptance. Of such experiences Schneider also says, "Simply because these phenomena are not measurable by existing methods need not lead to a rejection of the existence of the phenomena nor to a dogmatic stance of belief. As is true in science, nothing is proven; it is only understood, perhaps more clearly than previously." This intellectual insight, as helpful as it was for my understanding of how grief can be transformed, was not as convincing as Rose and Rita's acceptance of what they experienced.

Lessons for Caregivers

Mystery by its very nature implies something that is unexplainable and difficult to solve. Caregivers will hear a variety of stories from those who are going through the highly emotional experience of grief. The dying and their families may have experiences that they are at a loss to explain but that in some strange way help them move toward acceptance. What the caregivers are told may sound very strange and unbelievable, but it is not the place of the caregiver to question and introduce suspicion and doubt. It is enough that the story is something that is helping the person who is telling it to deal with her grief. The caregiver must be a gracious listener who celebrates the unexplainable mystery and affirms the meaning that is owned by the one who tells the story.

Caregivers may also witness the dying person in her last hours speaking to people who have been dead for many years, and speaking to them as if they were right there in the room or claiming to see them. These are mysterious moments for the caregiver to process and affirm. It is good to learn from the patient at that moment, to have her tell you as much as she can about what she is experiencing. In having her talk about what is bringing her contentment, we support her on her mysterious journey through the valley of the shadow.

I know that for both the daughter and the granddaughter of the deceased woman, the sweet smell of a pipe was a welcomed assurance that their loved one was at peace and with "Daddy." It was the kind of assurance they needed not only for that moment, but for their future memories, so that they would be able to look back on that moment with a measure of joy. I can only imagine that when either of them smells a smoking pipe it will mean something more to them than to all the others who are smelling the same scent.

chapter 25

A Child, a Ventilator, and a Choice

A terminal illness doesn't belong only to the one who is sick—it affects family members, friends, neighbors, and coworkers. Not unlike a still pond disturbed by a falling stone, an impending death sends ripples through all the relationships in the life of the dying.

—Maggie Callanan and Patricia Kelley

HOSPICE PROFESSIONALS, by nature of their job descriptions, confront death on a daily basis. Although each patient is unique, with each favoring his or her own personal plan of care, the staff is often able to recognize common dynamics that are present with the various diseases. Experience teaches us what to look for and how to anticipate and document the decline of each patient. To do this on a daily basis demands that staff members maintain a professional distance that enables them to fulfill their duties to the families and the dying patients. This professional control is hardest to maintain when the dying patient is a child. For me, it is even more difficult when the child arrives in our unit connected to a ventilator and the family has made the decision to remove the child from life support.

It was Saturday morning when I learned that Martina had been admitted to our unit earlier in the week. The girl was three years old and had been on a ventilator since birth. Following her birth, she remained in the hospital for five months and then was taken home, where she had been cared for by her parents for the past three years. I was informed that Martina's father was a pastor in a local congregation.

The nursing staff had been asked to plan to disconnect the ventilator on Monday morning. It was important to wait until Monday because Sunday was Father's Day, and Martina's father planned to conduct worship and preach that day. The staff decided to share a special Sunday lunch and a Father's Day cake with the family after the church service. Since Martina's parents were not in the unit when I was there on Saturday, I was not able to meet them until the following day.

That evening, I shared with my wife this family's circumstances, the difficulty of their choice, and the plans being made by the staff. As she listened to me, she was finishing sewing the binding on a small child's quilt. Without skipping a stitch, she said, "I want you to take this quilt and give it to the mother. I wasn't sure why or who I was making it for, but now I know."

The next day I met Martina's parents. After being introduced and sharing my concern for them, I gave Martina's mother the quilt as an expression of my wife's love and prayers for them. The woman was overcome with the joy of such an unexpected gift. When she had composed herself, she said, "You will never know how much this means to me. I prayed, only today, that God would give me a sign that what we were doing was within his will and that we would have people support us in our decision."

Needless to say, I, along with the nurse who was with me, was a bit choked up by the mother's words. I asked if we could talk after they finished their lunch, and Martina's parents quickly agreed. After lunch, we sat in the lounge together, and I asked if they would share with me what the past three years had been like and how difficult this decision was for them to make.

The mother began by saying, "God has been so good and given us so much of his grace. We are so grateful for Martina and for the love we share with her." She told me how the care of their child had become central to their home and all of their schedules.

I asked, "Have you had good support from your church?"

Her lips tightened and she shook her head from side to side, indicating that she hadn't had the support she had hoped for. She explained that she knew that it was hard for others to understand what she and her family were experiencing, but "if they would have just stopped by ..." She didn't complete her thought, but she didn't need to.

She shared with me that six months earlier they had discussed the matter of disconnecting the ventilator, but someone in the church had found out about it and confronted them with words that laid a heavy guilt trip on them. They stepped back from their decision and rethought it. Six months later, however, they came back to the same decision. They were at peace with the decision and felt it was God's will. Although they knew that not everyone would understand, they knew it was best. Their spiritual journey had brought them to a place of being accountable only to God.

The next day when I arrived, just before 6 a.m., Martina's mother was taking off the child's pajamas and dressing her in a pretty pink dress. She lovingly combed Martina's hair and braided it, tying the braids with two pink ribbons. The room was silent except for the sound of the ventilator that had been Martina's life source for the past three years.

The pediatric nurse arrived along with the pediatric physician. They had already met previously with the parents, but they reviewed the steps they were going to take. They explained the medicines that would be given to the girl to provide comfort in her last moments and what the family should expect when the ventilator was removed. As the doctor and nurse left the room I said to the parents, "Would this be a good time to offer a prayer together?"

The girl's father replied, "Prayer is always appropriate, especially now."

Following the prayer, Martina's father asked one of his other daughters to put on their favorite gospel CD. The song was "I

Can Only Imagine," a song in which the singer attempts to imagine what heaven will be like.

At 7 o'clock the physician indicated that it was time to remove the tube. When the process was complete, the father picked up his child, who was for the first time free of the tubing that had for three years tied her down, and placed her in her mother's arms. The sight of the mother sitting in the rocking chair cuddling her three-year-old gave a whole new meaning to "Madonna and Child."

For the next three hours the parents took turns holding their child while they listened to gospel music. The father read aloud from the book of Psalms. Staff members provided support by being present, but also from time to time left the room so that the family could have some time alone.

When Martina took her last breath, we were there with the family. The finality of the moment was overwhelming for all of us, and the staff provided individual comfort to each family member in the room. The waiting had ended.

The parents' faith enabled them to speak of their daughter as now being more whole than she had ever been. They spoke of her knowing more of God's love than any of us could in this life ever imagine. For the next two hours the mother cradled Martina in her arms. The mortuary was called and given a time when the parents would be ready for the body to be removed. Eventually, Martina's father gently took the child from her mother's arms, and they laid her on the bed. They hugged each other and then for some time cried together.

As I stood in the hallway looking in through the open door, I saw two parents who had traveled a difficult road but were claiming the promise that the God who had supplied all of their needs would continue to do so. I knew that the tears in my eyes were not so much for them but for myself. My wife and I have been blessed with three healthy children and eight healthy grandchildren, and I could only hope that if the same circumstances had been mine, my faith would sustain me in the same way.

Lessons for Caregivers

Caregivers, whether professionals or laypersons, face no more difficult situations than caring for families when a child is dying. The situation is even more difficult when an intentional decision must be made to turn off a ventilator. No amount of training can prepare a person for the emotional assault, and it might well be that such preparation is not even possible.

The best care-giving I have ever witnessed was provided by Martina's father and mother. Their three years of loving care included dealing with the pain caused by insensitive church members whose thoughtless remarks created undue anxiety and stress. It is important to learn from those people's thoughtless mistakes how hurtful it can be when a person makes judgments on others. What Martina's family needed was not criticism but understanding and a helpful presence, and yet no one in their church cared enough to drop by the house and offer support. I believe that speaks volumes about how hard it is to care in such difficult situations. It's far easier to gossip and criticize.

The caregivers who provided support for Martina's family did so in many different ways, and most often it was the little gestures and kindnesses that proved to the family that someone cared. Care-giving is rarely about highly developed plans and events that take a great deal of effort or money. It is usually the small, seemingly insignificant gesture that signals to the dying or the grieving that they are not alone.

A tear is not very large, but when it runs down the cheek of a caregiver and drops onto the shirt of a grieving father, it is a Niagara Falls of support. Caregivers who share not only their presence but also their tears sometimes discover an amazing strength as a result of how the family members respond.

Caregivers must also be honest in recognizing that their tears are not only for others but in many ways are for themselves. Any time that we identify with those who are dying and grieving and begin to transfer the possibility of their circumstances to our own personal relationships, we grieve personally. It is our ability to imagine such a personal loss in our own lives that stirs our emotions, and there is nothing wrong with this honest recognition, because it enables the caregiver to truly empathize, and it also reminds us of our own humanity.

After Words

The last chapters of this book focus not on dying patients but rather on people who are members of the caring profession and whose job it is to provide comfort to the dying and their families. These professionals are people who bring their own personal stories of human suffering with them to work every day, and out of their own faith experiences and their experiences of personal loss, they have become the "wounded healers."

chapter 26

Wounded Caregivers Need a Caregiver

❧❧❧❧❧❧❧❧❧❧❧❧❧❧❧❧❧❧❧❧❧❧❧❧❧❧❧❧❧❧❧❧❧❧❧❧

The great illusion of leadership is to think that man can be led out of the desert by someone who has never been there.

—*Henri J. M. Nouwen*

THE PALLIATIVE CARE units, as the chapters before have shown, are where our hospice team cares for patients who need specific pain control or respite care. In the units, staff members are busy meeting the physical, emotional, and spiritual needs of patients and their families. As each person carries out the expectations of his or her particular role, staff members often find themselves sitting at the unit desks charting their various activities or eating a meal together, and during such moments they share some of their personal lives with one another.

One particular day, one of the nurses was a bit tearful when she spoke about her sister's unplanned surgery. Her sister, who was 1,500 miles away, was being treated for colon cancer, and she had pain that needed to be dealt with, thus the need for surgery. After a couple of telephone calls had come into the unit regarding the nurse's sister, I became aware of this nurse's emotions. However, despite the pain she felt, she was still caring for her patients and seeing that their needs were met.

At one point I stopped the nurse, and looked her in the eyes, held out my arms, and hugged her. She immediately began to sob. When she had regained a bit of composure, I suggested that we sit together in the consultation room so that she could tell me about what she was going through and so we could pray together.

That nurse, like so many of her patients, had to face difficult questions regarding what kind of care to give to a loved one. She, like so many of her patient's families, was a very long distance from her loved one and felt the tension of making decisions between "being there or here." As she shared her personal pain with me and then with other staff members that day, we became very much aware that we who are caregivers are in no way exempt from the same human conditions and emotional pain of those who enter our unit to receive our caring.

Every staff person who was working on the unit that day was facing some life-and-death issues within his or her own family. We were discovering that what we have been trained to do professionally for others may provide a head knowledge for caring for others, but it doesn't negate the pain of personal experience. We all agreed that it is in the confronting of those crippling experiences of death and grief that we are better able to become the kind of caregivers who walk with others through their valleys of sorrow.

Lessons for Caregivers

Caregivers are not exempt from experiencing the physical, emotional, and spiritual pain that they are trained to care for in others. Admitting this is sometimes very difficult for caregivers, because they feel that it might in some way be unprofessional. But that is just the problem. I believe that compartmentalizing or separating the personal and the professional carries with it the risk of desensitizing a caregiver's feelings and seeing people as cases to be serviced rather than persons to be cared for. Many caregivers who do this do not know how to allow others to care for them.

Each caregiver has limited emotional strength and functions under the assumption that this limit is knowable and controllable. But when the unexpected happens at the most unlikely time, we hear those people referring to that moment as when "I lost it." What they are saying is that they lost control, and they apologize, as if doing so is a sign of weakness. What needs to be understood is that "losing it" is not so much a sign of weakness as a sign of humanness.

Such an experience provides a teachable moment. Out of such vulnerable experiences, caregivers discover their own humanness and become more genuine and honest with those for whom they care. Their experience does not give them the right to say, "I know how you feel," but it does help them to know the depth of others' feelings and to be more empathetic.

chapter 27

When Clergy Fear Being Caregivers

*I know that I do not know. In my work with people
who are dying, I often feel that I stand with them on
the threshold of the great mystery of time without end.
I do not pretend to have answers. It is not within my
capacity to discern ultimate meaning of life in the uni-
verse. I can only honor the mystery and hope to be of
some service to others.*

—Ira Byock

THE MOMENT WHEN a patient enters our hospice program is typ-
ically when his family begins to recognize the limitations of time.
Patients and family members begin a grieving process that will
place demands on their spiritual beliefs, and in those moments,
clergy have a unique opportunity to provide pastoral care.

Hospice of the Valley pastoral counselors provide a ministry to
patients and families, but that ministry is not intended to replace
or substitute for ministry that is provided by the local clergy.
When a patient or family has a relationship with a local clergyperson, we do all that we can to encourage networking with
that person so that the patient or family will be supported on their
spiritual journey.

There are clergy, however, who are not prepared to provide
such care to the dying and their families. Families expect that their
clergy will be prepared to help them, and many families are
helped, but others soon realize that their clergy are uneasy with
the circumstances of death. At such times, while the families are
polite and gracious in accepting whatever their clergy are prepared

to offer, they often request our pastoral counselors instead of their local clergy. When I talk with these families I sense a bit of disappointment that their clergy have not met their expectations. "He doesn't seem to be able to handle this" is a criticism I hear often.

I have been invited into such situations by families who have a strong religious faith and relationships with their local clergy. These families have been Jewish, Protestant, and Catholic, and all of them shared with me the same reason for asking for a hospice pastoral counselor: "Our clergy do not seem comfortable dealing with our needs." They go on to explain how the clergypersons are faithful in stopping by and "checking in" but are eager to simply read some Scripture, pray, and be on their way. They seem torn between "believing a miracle ought to be prayed for and just accepting the fact that we all die."

One afternoon when I called for a member of the clergy to come and visit a dying patient, he said to me, "You deal with this all the time. Why don't you handle it?" This was a clergyman who, simply by nature of how he clothed himself, would by his presence provide a very supportive and powerful symbol of God's love to the patient and his family. I reminded him of how important religious symbols were to his faith and how at the time of death a family finds those symbols to be very reassuring. I offered to meet with the family and pray with them, but explained that the clergyman's presence and his prayer would convey something more to them. He said, "OK. I'll get there as soon as I can." He arrived in the unit about thirty minutes later and went to be with the family. He offered prayers and Scriptures. The patient died about twenty minutes after the clergyman left the unit.

The family told me that they were very thankful that I was able to reach the clergyman and that he had come and stood with them in their final moments. That evening I called the clergyman again, and I thanked him for coming and shared how much it meant to the family that he had stood by the bedside with them. I suspect that he was thankful also, and that his conducting of that funeral service was more special to him because he had been there with the patient.

Some clergy do feel inadequate in ministering to dying patients and their families. They may simply lack experience or have not had the opportunity for any professional training for this type of situation. It is indeed a difficult topic to include in a seminary class on pastoral care, and as is the case with so many seminary classes, there is often a great deal of time between the classroom learning and the experience. All this notwithstanding, the conduct of caring is expected of the clergy, and it is important for them to do their best to live up to these expectations.

Lesson for Caregivers

It is difficult for me to be critical of people from my own profession, because I can remember my early years of being in pastoral ministry when I felt very insecure in caring for people who were dying and grieving. What I did about it is what others must also choose to do. First, I admitted to myself that I had a fear of those situations in which church members looked to me for something that I did not know how to give. Admitting the fear to myself was the biggest step. It was a step I had to take before I could convince myself that I needed help.

Next, I began to seek resources I could read that would help me broaden my understanding of how pastoral care should be performed in those situations. Back in the '70s there were far fewer resources than are available today, so I looked for other ways to learn as well. It was then that I enrolled in a Doctor of Ministry program and directed my final year of research in the area of grief recovery.

If clergy feel a lack of skills in the area of pastoral care, they need to look for continuing educational opportunities where they can receive the training that will help them. In addition, laypersons who are being trained as caregivers for congregations need support and feedback as part of their training.

Clergy are members of the "caring profession," and because of this, people who are suffering expect to be cared for by them. There is great disappointment when a clergyperson shows uneasiness or resistance to fulfilling this expectation. Honesty about this discomfort is the first step toward understanding what is lacking. The next response should be taking action to improve a caregiver's ability to truly care.

chapter 28

Practicing What We Preach

*The minister plays an important part on the caring
team of persons who are in key positions to relate to the
dying and their families. The minister's effectiveness in
the hospital room with the dying and in homes with the
grieving may depend on how well the teaching ministry
has been developed in the congregation. In the context
of preaching and educational classes in the program of
the church, the theological foundation is laid.*

—*William H. Griffith*

AS I HAVE OFTEN discovered during my thirty-five years of pastoral
ministry in the local church, it is important for the preacher to
"practice what is preached." It is not surprising that, over the past
five years of providing hope and support for others who are going
through the valley of the shadow, my family and I were also expected to take that journey ourselves. In a span of eleven months, three
members of my family—my mother and two sisters-in-law—died.
Our personal grief gave shape to our spiritual journeys.

Prior to these deaths and during the two years that I was writing this book, I was on several occasions asked to be a guest
preacher. As a retired pastor I have a "barrel" of sermons from
which I could have chosen, but I chose rather to use Scriptures
that speak about living life in the face of unwanted circumstances.
My choice was certainly conditioned by my weekly involvement
with dying patients and their families.

As I was preparing one particular sermon, I was reminded of an
old saying that is used in the training of young preachers: "Apply

yourself closely to the text. Apply the text closely to yourself." I began to ask myself, "How will I apply the texts I have recently preached? What will my spiritual journey look like if I apply myself closely to the text and let the text apply itself closely to me?"

The sermon was called "When the River Rises" and was based on Isaiah 43:1-13,18-19. My intent was to focus on four guideposts that would enable a person to journey beyond grief to faith. Through my many visits with dying patients and their families, I had come to discover that what so many of them were attempting to do was to find their way back from the devastating despair of losing what they valued most in life. I was drawn to the Isaiah text because for more than thirty years I had shared a poem at funeral services that was based on the text, and I wanted to know the truth of the text and not just the truth of the poem.

The text is a glimpse into the grief of Israel. The malignant hope of the people of Israel had caused them to conclude that their dreams were terminal. Those who once experienced "showers of blessings" were now experiencing the floodwaters of despair. They had been taken into exile and felt overwhelmed by their loss. That's exactly what my family and I felt when faced with a doctor's terminal diagnosis of one of our loved ones. I concluded that if this text was once meant to be a good word for others under these circumstances, then it must also be a good word for me. So I began my personal journey, stopping long enough at each guidepost to reflect and hope.

Guidepost #1: God Knows Us

The first guidepost is a reminder that God knows us personally. Verse 1 says, "Fear not, for I have redeemed you; / I have summoned you by name; you are mine" (NIV). We are so much like Israel in that we are not always as obedient as we ought to be about living a good life. I have found that people who are dying often review their lives and remember the things they have done that they should not have done. They suffer from the guilt and the fear that they have gone beyond God's ability or willingness to redeem them. People with such a hopeless feeling need to hear again the word spoken in this text: "Fear not, for I have redeemed you; / I have summoned you by name; you are mine."

There is no one I know who has believed this text more than my mother. It's not a verse I ever heard her mention, but I know that she valued it because she had it underlined in her Bible. Her spiritual journey was shaped by her devotion to reading and understanding the Bible. At her memorial service, tributes were offered by her great-grandson, her grandson, and me. The common theme was her tattered, worn Bible. It was from that Bible that her grandson read the Scriptures, and he was quick to mention that it was at least the third Bible she had worn out during her lifetime.

My mother died at age eighty-eight while being cared for in a comfort care facility. During her final years, I traveled from Arizona to Rochester, New York, three or four times a year to visit with her. It was never difficult for me to leave her bedside and make my return flight home, because I knew that the hope by which she had lived had prepared her to die. She knew the truth of Isaiah's words, which affirmed for her that God had redeemed her. Knowing that gave me comfort and hope.

Guidepost #2: God Is with Us

The second guidepost in the journey from grief to comfort is the assurance that God is always with us. God is actually in the *middle* of our despair. Verse 2 reads,

> *When you pass through the waters,*
> *I will be with you;*
> *and when you pass through the rivers,*
> *they will not sweep over you.*
> *When you walk through the fire,*
> *you will not be burned;*
> *the flames will not set you ablaze.*

I am the first to admit that it's much easier "to talk the talk than to walk the walk." It's much easier for me to sit by the bed of a dying patient who is struggling with the unfairness of her situation and offer her some words of hope and consolation than it is for me to remember those same words when I am told that one of my own family members has been diagnosed with a terminal illness. Being told by someone at such a time that God hasn't deserted me may be a true and important reminder, but it doesn't magically make the sense of unfairness or overwhelming despair go away.

Having two sisters-in-law, Clarice and Sarah, die less that a year ago from the time of this writing caused me to be more aware of how very inadequate mere words can be to ease and soften the ache and void that is felt when a loved one is dying. Loss of life cannot be verbally massaged and explained into becoming more acceptable.

For me, I knew God was in the midst of our despair because there were people who were "with us," and by their presence we knew that we were not alone. My spiritual journey had prior experiences of loss, and by remembering them I was able to put the present loss into the larger picture. This helped me see that God had been there in the past loss, and therefore I was able to be confident that God was somewhere in my present despair. When I came to understand this, the promises from the Scriptures began to reshape my present, and I began to accept them as comforting words. The biblical image of being in a river that is overflowing its banks and needing to be reassured that there's someone in there with me who's going to get me through it becomes an image of hope that helps me proceed on my journey.

As my family and I were experiencing the rising waters of grief and sorrow, we experienced a godly presence in the form of two Episcopal priests who were the pastors of the church that Clarice and Sarah attended. They were there at the bedside during both our loved ones' dying hours, providing words and sacraments to affirm each of their spiritual journeys. Their presence and prayers also provided the needed comfort and support for each member of our family. It is that ministry of a godly presence that reassures us that the waters will not overflow.

Guidepost #3: God Loves Us As We Are

The third guidepost is the reminder that God loves us as we are. Verse 4 says, "You are precious and honored in my sight, / and because *I love you* ..." (emphasis added).

Experiencing loss creates an anxiety and stress that often causes us to direct our anger toward God. I've counseled people who expressed that anger in harsh words; some have even cursed God. It's an honest expression of what a person feels, and it is good for those feelings to be expressed. God is big enough and has been around long enough to handle our anger. What is amazing is that anyone against whom we are expressing such hostilities would want us to know that we are still loved. God doesn't seem to take our anger personally and is mostly concerned about our well-being. In spite of our perception of a distant God, God is nearer than we dare believe, and God loves us.

Guidepost #4: God Calls Us Onward

The fourth guidepost reminds us that God calls us to a future that is brighter than the past. Verses 18 and 19 say, "Forget the former things; / do not dwell on the past. / See I am doing a new thing!" Here again, it's easier said than done. It's easier to believe such a statement for someone else's situation than it is to claim it for one's own situation. It is always easier to mouth platitudes and clichés in an attempt to ease someone else's pain than to believe them for ourselves. How much we are willing to believe those words depends on how fully they were proven to be true after our last experience with loss.

However, having a "pity party" hinders our ability to discover the new thing that God wants to do for us. That new thing will not just show up while we lock ourselves in our bedrooms. The new thing demands that we do our part to invest in something outside of ourselves. We do so not to deny our pain but to see our pain within the larger perspective of life. This proclaims trust that God will help us see it as he sees it. The goal is not so much to minimize our pain but to reclaim and maximize our potential.

It was good for me to have prepared and preached a sermon from this text, not only because someone in the congregation may have been encouraged by hearing it, but because the time would come when I would have to practice what I preached.

Lessons for Caregivers

I have always been amazed at how often the text I chose for a particular Sunday sermon ended up addressing an issue that I also had to face that week in some area of my relationships. It demanded honesty and vulnerability to stand in the pulpit and proclaim a word from God that I had to practice myself.

In this final chapter, I have attempted to share how I have practiced what I have preached. Preachers, teachers, and caregivers may easily conclude that the message they offer is good for others, but fail to discover and apply the same truths to their own lives. My thirty-five years of preaching and teaching about death, grief, faith, and end-of-life issues were rarely personally tested until I was completing the writing of this book. Being required to practice what I had been preaching has reaffirmed the value of understanding how faith can be proclaimed and even renewed amidst the reality of death and grief.

For Reflection

∎∎

Introduction

1. Do you agree with the author that people are very uncomfortable with redefining their relationship with someone whose diagnosis is terminal? Have you ever had to redefine such a relationship?

2. What scares you the most about having to deal with such an uncomfortable situation?

3. Was there a time when you just wanted someone to be with you and did not expect him or her to have answers? If you feel comfortable doing so, share this with others.

4. Is "just being with" someone difficult for you? If so, why?

5. Why do you think that being honest in our conversation with a dying person so difficult?

6. What makes redefining hope so important for the dying? Have you any examples of how you've done this with others or of how others have helped you do it?

Chapter 1: From Restlessness to Peace

1. Reread the quote at the beginning of this chapter. How does this quote summarize the point of this chapter?

2. What is the significance of recognizing something such as the bedroom furniture that was being stored in the living room?

3. Why was it appropriate to invite John's wife to stay and be a part of the conversation?

4. How did the author help John get in touch with the fact that waiting wasn't easy for most people? How did this help John?

5. What is your opinion about the bridge the author provided to the Scriptures? Was it appropriate? Why or why not?

6. What did the author do before leaving that showed concern for the family? Why was that important?

Chapter 2: The Mysterious Power of Hope

1. Reread the quote at the beginning of this chapter. Can you think of times or places when you've experienced mystery? Did anything give you a sense of being closer to God?

2. How was Tom's question different from John's in Chapter 1?

3. What did the author say that demonstrated honesty in answering Tom's question?

4. What was the key question Tom was asked that put him in touch with his will to live a bit longer? What process did Tom enter into by answering this question?

5. Have you known someone who was dying but showed some sign of holding on until a special event or occasion?

Chapter 3: Confession Cleans the Slate

1. Reread the quote at the beginning of this chapter. Do you agree that "death gives life to the God-question"? Why or why not?

2. How does the author's use of the journey image enable Kelly to talk about her spirituality?

3. Why was the silence between Kelly and the author so powerful? What was communicated in their silence? Do you find silence difficult?

4. What was communicated in the touch that took place between them? Are you comfortable using touch as a means of caring?

5. How does Kelly's experience teach us that reconciliation, both with God and with others, can make death more peaceful?

6. For those who feel as hopeless as Kelley does, what medicine does the author suggest the caregiver can offer?

Chapter 4: Learning to See the Heart

1. Reread the quote at the beginning of this chapter. For what can the dying and their families offer thanks when they are overwhelmed with grief and sorrow? How does it help?

2. What was the first lesson the author learned from his experience with Phil's friends at the memorial service? Have you discovered the need from time to time to relearn this lesson?

3. What was another lesson the author learned?

4. How would you describe the sense of community that was being experienced by those who attended Phil's memorial service? Is this community anything like what people in a faith community are meant to experience?

5. What are some ways caregivers can make sure that friends and their contributions are not forgotten?

Chapter 5: Respecting the Hearing of the Dying

1. Reread the quote at the beginning of this chapter. Just how are we all teachers for one another as we face our own dying, and how does that define how we will relate to those who are dying?

2. How do you feel about visiting a person who is non-responsive? Do you feel useless, helpless?

3. Have you ever talked with, read to, or prayed with a non-responsive dying person? If not, why not? If so, what was the experience like?

4. What did the author do that showed that he believed what he says about dying patients having the potential to hear although they show no signs of being responsive?

5. Do you think we rightly assume that people want someone with them when they die? Do you know anyone who carries the regret of not being present at the time of someone's death?

6. What does the possibility that a non-responsive person can hear teach us about what we should talk about by the bedside?

Chapter 6: Taking a Child's Grief Seriously

1. Reread the quote at the beginning of this chapter. How does this quote put us in touch with our humanity and prepare us to be better caregivers?

2. Name one way that adults do a poor job of teaching children about death and grief? How did Jessica's mother do this?

3. What can we assume about the theology that was taught to Jessica during her time of grief? Can theology be a denial on the part of adults to deal with emotions?

4. How did the author get Jessica to be in touch with her feelings of loss and grief without discussing death?

5. How did he identify with her feelings of sadness and get her to begin to realize that she's not alone?

6. Why did the author tell Jessica a story? Do you know any stories that you could tell a child that would help him or her process sadness and grief?

Chapter 7: Faith-Based Denial

1. Reread the quote at the beginning of this chapter. Given the near-universal teaching of the importance of "getting one's house in order" before one dies, how can we be sensitive to the dying person's fears?

2. How would you answer the author's question: "Can such a person be in denial if she is bold enough to verbalize it? Is the admission of denial at some level a recognition of the reality of what is being denied?"

3. How did the author begin his conversation with this patient? What do you imagine led him to begin this way?

4. How did the author refocus when the patient signaled an end to the discussion about theology?

5. How important is it to clarify the words we use with the dying when the words may have multiple meanings? What does this say about the need to be sensitive to symbolic language used by the patient?

6. How can denial of dying be thought of as a form of affirming one's faith? Have you ever known anyone who was dying but was told that he or she just had to have more faith and God would heal him or her?

Chapter 8: Faith Traditions That Care

1. Reread the quote at the beginning of this chapter. If we believe that death confronts people with the question of "ultimate meaning," how should this help us to be sensitive to the dying?

2. What was the defining dynamic of the community that was gathered at the dying patient's bedside? How might a caregiver facilitate this dynamic under other circumstances?

3. Would you have handled the situation the way the author did, or would you have taken a more active role? What important principle was the author practicing by his response?

4. Reflect on experiences you have had in which you have shared a special moment of community with people who were joined by common values and beliefs.

Chapter 9: Faith, Unanswered Prayer, and God's Will

1. Reread the quote at the beginning of this chapter. Why will believing these words make us better caregivers?

2. How usual or unusual is it for a person not only to ask God for a sign but to specify what that sign ought to be?

3. What were the two sides of the tension that pulled at Michael as he attempted to deal with his wife's condition? What are the pros and cons of each side?

4. How would you have felt if you were Michael and a white dove appeared just as you prayed?

5. Was the author being too hard on Michael when he continued to remind him of the nature of the disease? Why or why not?

6. What was the strength of Michael's hope that no doubt helped him to define his future after his wife died?

7. Can you think of a loving way to affirm one's faith, but also to confront their denial?

Chapter 10: When God Appears to Someone

1. Reread the quote at the beginning of this chapter. What do you think of the analogy of life being like a sailing ship that departs from a shore that is familiar and arrives at another that is unseen?

2. What would be your first thought upon hearing someone say that God had appeared to him?

3. What can we learn from the way the author paid attention to the ring on Eldon's hand?

4. Have you ever had an experience that you hesitated to share because it may made you appear to be "wacko" or at least caused a look of suspicion on another's face?

5. What did Eldon say that showed that he had assurance and peace regarding his condition?

6. If you were to create a symbol to define the story of your spiritual journey, what would that symbol be?

7. Does Eldon's experience surprise you in any way?

Chapter 11: A Spiritually Disturbed Christian

1. Reread the quote at the beginning of this chapter. How do we listen to the pain?

2. What did Barbara say that got the author's attention? How important is it to listen to the expressions of a dying person to discover what he or she needs most from a caregiver?

3. Have you known anyone who has had a near-death experience? How was that person different after the experience?

4. How was the author's response to Barbara an example of the importance of honesty in care-giving?

Chapter 12: Emotional and Spiritual Pain Levels

1. Reread the quote at the beginning of this chapter. Do you fear death? If you answer yes and you are also uncomfortable with caring for the dying and grieving, do you think that your fear may be the cause?

2. Who were the sensitive caregivers who connected Rick to the author? How did they act on their sensitivity?

3. What relationships were creating Rick's emotional pain?

4. How did Rick's inability to forget contribute to his spiritual pain?

5. Would you have responded differently at any point? If so, how?

Chapter 13: The Fear of Grieving Alone

1. Reread the quote at the beginning of this chapter. Have you or someone you know experienced the emotion of this quote?

2. What basic human need was met for the grieving fifteen-year-old mother?

3. What kind of person can meet this kind of need? Where does a person learn how to care for another in this way?

4. What was the mother grieving about?

5. If the "why" question were answered for her, would the mother's grief remain?

Chapter 14: Honor the Care Receiver's Faith

1. Reread the quote at the beginning of this chapter. What for you are the key words in this quote?

2. What signal did the author receive that indicated that his presence with the patient was appreciated and sufficient?

3. What did the author learn when he asked whether Jacob had assurance of God's love and care? Is there a different question you would have asked?

4. How would you describe the dynamic that took place over the next hour they shared together?

5. Would you have concluded the visit any differently? If so, how?

Chapter 15: Forgiveness Minimizes the Regrets

1. Reread the quote at the beginning of this chapter. When good people ask you why bad things happen to them, do you have an answer?

2. What signal did Lois send to those around her? How were those caring for her sensitive to the best way to help her?

3. What did the author do to identify the emotion that he saw in Lois? Once such an emotion is identified, what must be done with it?

4. What was the risk Lois had to take?

5. What do we learn from Lois and her daughter, Sarah, about assuming that all is well between the dying and those who are their primary caregivers?

6. How was this a bittersweet experience for Lois? Have you ever shared a similar experience?

Chapter 16: When Feelings Undermine Faith

1. Reread the quote at the beginning of this chapter. How do you respond to people who apologize for their tears and overwhelming grief?

2. Why was the author's opening invitation, "Talk to me, tell me what you've been thinking," a good way to begin?

3. What did Jane quickly reveal regarding her internal anxiousness that gave the author a clue not only to her need but also to how he might respond?

4. Why was using Scripture appropriate in responding to Jane?

5. Can you think of a time when your feelings called your faith into question?

6. What did Jane, who was a religious person, teach caregivers not to assume?

Chapter 17: Caring for the Dying Agnostic

1. Reread the quote at the beginning of this chapter. How does it define a caregiver's experience?

2. What was there about the way the author approached Joan that set the tone for their relationship?

3. Why was detecting Joan's fears and mentioning them to her a legitimate way to care for her?

4. What conclusion did Joan make, based on her values and beliefs, about others in her situation?

5. What do you think about the author's personal question to her? What did she reveal by her response and through the discussion that followed?

6. How important was the author's promise to come back and talk more the next day?

7. Why is asking a person permission to pray for him or her an important thing?

Chapter 18: The Vertical and Horizontal Relationships Are Important

1. Reread the quote at the beginning of this chapter. What would you hope to be doing at the time of your death?

2. What lesson does Lela teach us about the mind of someone who is dying?

3. Was Lela at peace with God?

4. How did talking about the white dove provide an opening for meaningful sharing? Would you have done it differently?

5. Why wasn't Lela ready to die? How was she encouraged to get ready?

Chapter 19: Helping a Grieving Family

1. Reread the quote at the beginning of this chapter. What lesson is here for caregivers?

2. What were some reasons for asking the family to share stories about their mother's life as they gathered in the room where she had died?

3. How has a deceased member of your family left you with an important legacy? Who was that member, and what did he or she leave you?

4. Would you say that parents today are more or less intentional than the Navajo mother was at passing on their values and beliefs? Why?

5. Can you think of a poem, saying, or writing that you would like to sum up your life?

Chapter 20: Moving from Doubt to Faith

1. Reread the quote at the beginning of this chapter. What ways or symbols help you memorialize a loved one who is now deceased?

2. How would you describe the difference in the relationships of the people in this family and those of the Navajo family in the previous chapter?

3. What did the wording of the son's question reveal about his theology? How did this help the author know where the son was coming from?

4. Why do you imagine that the adult children were asked to leave the room but the husband was asked to remain?

5. In what way did the author ease into the religious nature of his visit? What do we learn from this approach?

6. How well do you know the religious values of those nearest to you? Do they know yours?

7. What lessons do caregivers learn about also relating to family members of those who are dying?

Chapter 21: The Fear of God's Rejection Too

1. Reread the quote at the beginning of this chapter. Who is the "we" in this quote, and what is their role with the dying and family members?

2. What was troubling Michael enough that he asked for a visit from a pastoral counselor?

3. What was the concern that Michael shares with many others who are dying?

4. What good news eased Michael's troubled spirit?

5. Would being a caregiver for a dying AIDS patient be difficult for you? If so, why?

Chapter 22: From Agitation to Confession

1. Reread the quote at the beginning of this chapter. What realization must be accepted to be a good caregiver?

2. What is the simple act of caring that Francis's daughter-in-law offered him?

3. What gave her the insight and hope that this act might be what Francis needed?

4. How is it that what we see in a skilled nursing facility may prevent us from providing what a patient needs?

Chapter 23: When the One Dying Is a Personal Friend

1. Reread the quote at the beginning of this chapter. What conversations might you have in interacting with a dying person based on the wisdom offered in this quote?

2. How did Robin's choice of words indicate his comfort level for communication about his hopes and fears?

3. What statement did Robin make that signaled that he had reached a point of acceptance?

4. Robin's basic need was not different from that of most people who are dying. How did he convey that need?

5. How did talking about planting trees provide Robin with an instant answer to his question? What might this say about the importance of using illustrations to make a serious point?

6. How was Robin also a wonderful caregiver himself? What lesson does he teach caregivers about listening for the unfinished business of those who are dying?

Chapter 24: Comfort Is Not Always Explainable

1. Reread the quote at the beginning of this chapter. Do you agree or disagree with the opening sentence?

2. How does the amount of time that a person knows about a terminal diagnosis help that person process his or her grief? What was so shocking to the daughter regarding her mother's death?

3. How did the author's question regarding the family's special memories of the deceased woman help them?

4. What statement did the daughter express that showed that she was attempting to move toward acceptance?

5. How valid was the family's interpretation of what the pipe smell meant to them?

Chapter 25: A Child, a Ventilator, and a Choice

1. Reread the quote at the beginning of this chapter. Does your own experience validate this quote? Can you identify the ripples of grief that affected you as a family member, friend, neighbor, or coworker?

2. Identify the various ways that individuals cared for this family during those few days together in the hospice.

3. How did the attitudes and beliefs of others impact the struggle the parents had to make? How did the source of those attitudes complicate their decision-making?

4. What gave the parents the most peace about making such a difficult decision?

5. When you've experienced the emotion of grief, have you been able to discern whether the grief is over another person's loss or for the potential of a loss of your own?

Chapter 26: Crippled Caregivers Need a Caregiver

1. Reread the quote at the beginning of this chapter. Do you agree with this quote? If so, why or why not?

2. What experiences have you had that better prepare you to feel the pain of the one for whom you are caring?

3. Have you ever had to put your personal emotions aside to meet another's need?

4. Why is it not appropriate to say to another grieving person, "I know how you feel"?

Chapter 27: When Clergy Fear Being Caregivers

1. Reread the quote at the beginning of this chapter. Can you think of a time when you knew the truth of this quote because you did not have the answers?

2. What is the struggle that clergy and other religious persons have in dealing with the reality of the dying process?

3. How can they come to terms with their struggle?

4. How might group sessions in a faith community that is focused on death and grief assist both the clergy and the congregation?

Chapter 28: Practicing What We Preach

1. Reread the quote at the beginning of this chapter. Which of the three lessons mentioned in the introduction of this book does this quote echo? Why is that lesson difficult to practice?

2. What life experience have you had that relates to the possibility of "the waters overflowing"?

3. What for you is the key emphasis shared in this sermon that you hope to remember when grief suddenly overwhelms you? How can knowing this better help you care for others?

4. Remember a personal loss and identify how you were assured that God was with you.

5. How do you respond to the statement that we must "invest in something outside of ourselves ... not to deny our pain but to put our pain in the larger perspective of life"? Have you had to do that?

Quotation Sources

1   Earl A. Grollman, *Living When a Loved One Has Died* (Boston: Beacon Press, 1977), 106.
2   Peter J. Gomes, *The Good Book: Reading the Bible with Mind and Heart* (New York: HarperCollinsPublishers, 1996), 327.
3   Peter J. Kreeft, *Love Is Stronger Than Death* (San Francisco: Harper and Row Publishers, 1979), xviii.
4   William H. Griffith, from the sermon "When Terror Strikes," preached at the Desert Hills Presbyterian Church, Scottsdale, AZ, on July 21, 2002.
5   As found in Roger Lipsey, "How Long, O Lord?" *Parabola,* Volume 27, Number 2, May 2002, 34.
6   J. Donald Bane, et al., eds., *Death and Ministry: Pastoral Care of the Dying and the Bereaved* (New York: Seabury Press, 1975), vii.
7   Megory Anderson, *Sacred Dying: Creating Rituals for Embracing the End of Life* (New York: Marlowe & Company, 2001), 113.
8   Richard W. Doss, *The Last Enemy: A Christian Understanding of Death* (New York: Harper & Row, 1974), xiii.
9   Madeleine L'Engle, *Sold Into Egypt: Joseph's Journey into Human Being* (Wheaton, IL: Harold Shaw, 1989), 199.
10 Peter J. Kreeft, *Love Is Stronger Than Death* (San Francisco: Harper and Row Publishers, 1979), 65.
11 As found in Kenneth J. Doka, ed., with Joyce Davidson, *Living With Grief When Illness Is Prolonged* (Washington, DC: Hospice Foundation of America, 1977), 181.

12 Gladys M. Hunt, *The Christian Way of Death* (Grand Rapids, MI: Zondervan, 1971), 73.

13 Earl A. Grollman, "Spiritual Support After Sudden Loss" in *Living With Grief After Sudden Loss,* edited by Kenneth J. Doka (Washington, DC: Hospice Foundation of America and Bristol, PA: Taylor & Francis Publishers, 1996), 106.

14 Deuteronomy 31:8.

15 Earl A. Grollman, "Spiritual Support After Sudden Loss" in *Living With Grief After Sudden Loss,* edited by Kenneth J. Doka (Washington, DC: Hospice Foundation of America and Bristol, PA: Taylor & Francis Publishers, 1996), 105.

16 James L. Mayfield, *Discovering Grace in Grief* (Nashville: Upper Room Books, 1994), 34.

17 R. F. Smith Jr., *Sit Down, God ... I'm Angry* (Valley Forge, PA: Judson Press, 1997), 137.

18 Philip Yancey, *Where Is God When It Hurts?* (Grand Rapids, MI: Zondervan, 1977), 49.

19 Herbert N. Conley, *Living & Dying Gracefully* (New York: Paulist Press, 1979), 67.

20 Earl A. Grollman, *Living When a Loved One Has Died* (Beacon Press, Boston 1977), 105.

21 Elisabeth Kübler-Ross, *On Death and Dying* (New York: Macmillan Publishing, 1969), 142.

22 Earl A. Grollman, ed., *Concerning Death: A Practical Guide for the Living* (Boston: Beacon Press, 1974), xiv.

23 Ira Byock, *Dying Well: The Prospect for Growth at the End of Life* (New York: Riverhead Books, 1997), 238.

24 James L. Mayfield, *Discovering Grace in Grief* (Nashville: Upper Room Books, 1994), 85.

25 Maggie Callanan and Patricia Kelley, *Final Gifts: Understanding the Special Awareness, Needs, and Communications of the Dying* (New York: Bantam Books, 1992), 2.

26 Henri J. M. Nouwen, *The Wounded Healer,* quoted in *A*

Guide to Prayer for Ministers and Other Servants by Rueben Job and Norman Shawchuck (Nashville: The Upper Room, 1983), 200.

27 Ira Byock, *The Four Things That Matter Most: A Book About Living* (New York: Free Press, 2004), 194.

28 William H. Griffith, *Confronting Death* (Valley Forge, PA: Judson Press, 1977), 13.

About the Author

WILLIAM H. GRIFFITH is an ordained American Baptist clergyman who was on the Hospice of the Valley pastoral counseling staff in Phoenix, Arizona, from 1999–2004. He is presently a member of the chaplaincy staff of Hospice of South Central Indiana, Inc. He is pastor emeritus of The First Baptist Church of Terre Haute, Indiana, and a graduate of Houghton College (B.A.) and Gordon Conwell Theological Seminary (M.Div.). In 1975 he received his D.Min. in grief recovery from Eastern Baptist Theological Seminary in Philadelphia, Pennsylvania. He is the author of the book *Confronting Death,* published by Judson Press.

Griffith has held senior pastoral positions in Woodbury, New Jersey; Columbus, Indiana; and Terre Haute, Indiana. He has also served as chaplain of the Four Seasons Retirement Center in Columbus, Indiana, as a volunteer chaplain with Bartholomew County Hospice from 1980–1982, and as a bereavement support facilitator at the Union hospital in Terre Haute, Indiana.